# SpringerBriefs in Information Systems

*Series editor*

Jörg Becker, Münster, Germany

For further volumes:
http://www.springer.com/series/10189

Ralf Plattfaut

# Process-Oriented Dynamic Capabilities

## Framework Development, Empirical Applications and Methodological Support

 Springer

Ralf Plattfaut
European Research Center for Information
   Systems
Westfälische Wilhelms-Universität
   Münster
Münster
Germany

ISSN 2192-4929          ISSN 2192-4937   (electronic)
ISBN 978-3-319-03250-4     ISBN 978-3-319-03251-1   (eBook)
DOI 10.1007/978-3-319-03251-1
Springer Cham Heidelberg New York Dordrecht London

Library of Congress Control Number: 2013953687

Printed on acid-free paper

Springer is part of Springer Science+Business Media (www.springer.com)

# Foreword

The innovation of services becomes increasingly important for economic development world-wide. On the one hand, companies in manufacturing industries extend their product portfolio with new services to generate further income streams and profits. On the other hand, the relevance of the pure service sector for Western economies is increasing, too. Multiple empirical studies underline the importance of service innovation for business growth. However, previous studies also show that the topic of service innovation needs further theoretical work. This is true for the related area of process management, too. Next to the theoretical work, further design-oriented research is needed. Literature shows a clear demand for specific methods and tools that support service innovation in practice. Here, especially the information-reuse between the phases of idea generation, concept development, and solution implementation is in the focus.

With this SpringerBrief, Ralf Plattfaut presents findings of his work with regards to the mentioned research gaps. The contributions he offers are threefold. First, after a thorough review of the relevant literature, he presents a conceptual framework that can be used to study process-oriented dynamic capabilities such as service innovation of process management. Second, he evaluates this framework with the help of various qualitative and quantitative studies. Third, he presents results of design-oriented research in term of a new method for service innovation and a corresponding technological artifact.

The results have been achieved in practice-oriented research projects funded by the German Federal Ministry of Education and Research. Like these projects, this SpringerBrief is an example for Information Systems research that is interesting for both practitioners and scholars.

Münster, August 2013                                                                 Jörg Becker

# Acknowledgments

When I started my undergraduate studies in Information Systems at the University of Münster several years ago, even the idea of going for a Ph.D. was far away. Now, after several years at University, I am able to present this SpringerBrief based on the introductory chapters of my cumulative doctoral thesis (article thesis).[1]

Most of the research results were achieved in the projects "Kollaboratives prozessorientiertes Produktivitätsmanagement von Dienstleistungen (KollaPro)",[2] "Steigerung von Innovationsfähigkeit im demografischen Wandel durch die Integration sozialer Medien und IT-gestützter Geschäftsprozesse (WeChange)",[3] "Networked Service Society (NSS)",[4] and "Electronic Government in einer alternden Gesellschaft—Policies, Projekte, Potenziale (AgeGov)".[5] While the first three projects are funded by the German Federal Ministry of Education and Research (Bundesministerium für Bildung und Forschung), the last one is funded by the VolkswagenStiftung.

In such settings, research is a collaborative endeavor: I worked together with several colleagues from the University of Münster, other universities, and private companies. My research was also supported by students and research assistants. I would like to express my gratitude to them: Thank you! Moreover, I would like to thank some people outside the academic world. Steffi, thank you for the motivation, encouragement, and love. My friends, thank you for keeping me sane and happy. My parents and brothers were and are giving me their unconditional support. I cannot thank you enough.

Münster, August 2013                                                      Ralf Plattfaut

---

[1] As such, this SpringerBrief presents a new organization of research results obtained on the topic of process-oriented dynamic capabilities. I tried to reference the original articles wherever needed.

[2] Collaborative process-oriented productivity management of services, http://www.kollapro.net (promotional reference 01FL10004).

[3] Building innovation capabilities in times of demographic change through the integration of social media and IT-supported business processes, http://www.projectwechange.de (promotional reference 01HH11059).

[4] http://www.networkedservicesociety.net (promotional reference APR 10/805).

[5] Electronic government in aging societies—policies, projects, potentials, http://www.agegov.org.

# Contents

# Abbreviations

| | |
|---|---|
| AIS | Association for Information Systems |
| AMCIS | Americas Conference on Information Systems |
| BMC | Business Model Canvas |
| BPM | Business Process Management |
| CEO | Chief Executive Officer |
| CIO | Chief Information Officer |
| CRM | Customer Relationship Management |
| DSL | Digital Subscriber Line |
| ERP | Enterprise Resource Planning |
| EU | European Union |
| IPTV | Internet Protocol Television |
| IS | Information Systems |
| IT | Information Technology |
| PLS | Partial Least Squares |
| PLS-SEM | Partial Least Squares Structural Equation Modeling |
| RBV | Resource-based View |
| RQ | Research Question |
| SEM | Structural Equation Modeling |
| SME | Small and Medium-sized Enterprise |
| TQM | Total Quality Management |
| VDSL | Very-high-bit-rate Digital Subscriber Line |
| VRIN | Valuable, Rare, Imperfectly Imitable, and Non-substitutable |

# Chapter 1
# Exposition

## 1.1 Motivation

In today's networked service society, service innovation becomes increasingly important. In 2012, the creation of new services was among the top five global business strategies (Gartner Inc. 2012). One reason for this is the importance of service innovation for business growth: 25 % of Chief Executive Officers (CEOs) from leading companies argue that new product or service development is the main opportunity for growth in 2013 (PwC 2013). This perception is mirrored by recent publications of the European Union (EU): "Service innovation can play an important role in industrial policy because it has the potential to transform Europe's businesses, thus making a strong contribution to the Europe 2020 strategy for smart, sustainable and inclusive growth." (Enterprise and Industry Magazine 2011). However, not all organizations are fully able to create new services in an efficient and effective way. Exemplarily, Chief Information Officers (CIOs) from leading organizations see potential for improving the innovation-friendliness of their organizational culture. They ranked the implementation of corresponding measures as their second most important priority for 2013 (Loftus 2013). As such, it can be argued that practitioners have seen the need to create new services and build their service innovation capabilities accordingly.

Scientific literature agrees with these decision makers. Berry et al. (2006, p. 56) argue that it is only naturally "that companies are constantly seeking to provide better services, regardless of whether they are in a 'pure' service business or in a manufacturing industry that must increasingly rely on its service operations for continued profitability." According to a more recent study, the organizational "ability [...] to provide its customers with innovative products and services will be critical to sustainable success in the twenty-first century." (Maleyeff 2011, p. 111) Thus, scientific literature underlines the need to develop the right capabilities for service innovation.

The concept of service innovation shares several traits with the concept of process innovation (Hipp et al. 2000), or, more generally, Business Process Management (BPM). According to Katzan (2008), an important characteristic

R. Plattfaut, *Process-Oriented Dynamic Capabilities*, SpringerBriefs in Information Systems, DOI: 10.1007/978-3-319-03251-1_1, © The Author(s) 2014

of services is their process nature. Other authors go further and argue that services can be understood as processes (Bitner et al. 2008). With regards to service innovation, Maleyeff argues that it is closely related to process innovation and that it can be achieved with concepts such as Total Quality Management (TQM), Six Sigma, or Lean Management (2011), which are all means to achieve process innovation, too. Again, most organizations lack process innovation or BPM capabilities: About 75 % of all CIOs argue that their Information Technology (IT) department is currently lacking skills to deliver business process improvements (Gartner Inc. 2012).

As such, both BPM and service innovation can be understood as the capabilities of an organization to create innovations with regards to processes. BPM is a holistic management approach that applies measures of punctuated and incremental change with the aim of business process improvement (Armistead and Machin 1997, 1998; Pritchard and Armistead 1999; Rosemann et al. 2006; Zairi 1997). Thus, BPM can be defined as an organization's ability to change (e.g., integrate, build, reconfigure, improve, adapt, adjust, refresh, renew, etc.) the organization's business processes (Niehaves et al. 2010). While conceptually related, service innovation is an organization's ability to change the organization's services (or: service processes) (Pöppelbuß et al. 2011) and, thus, requires comparable (but distinct) methods, tools, and activities.

From a theoretical perspective, it is without doubt that BPM research (and Information Systems (IS) research in general) often lags behind practice (Melão and Pidd 2000). Scholars have argued that research is currently still on the way towards BPM theory and further work is needed (Smart et al. 2009). The same can be said about service innovation: Despite early efforts in theorizing in the field of service innovation, further theory development is needed (Bullinger et al. 2003; Hipp et al. 2000; Maglio and Spohrer 2007; Tether 2002). As service innovation is closely related to BPM, a theoretical framework that helps understanding BPM would also foster service innovation understanding.

Such a theoretical framework should form the basis for the development of new methods and tools used to support BPM and service innovation. Especially for service innovation, such methods and tools are still lacking (Bullinger et al. 2003). Bullinger et al. argue that these methods and tools should support the three distinct steps of (a) brainstorming and idea appraisal, (b) concept elaboration, and (c) service implementation (2003).

## 1.2  Problem Statement and Research Questions

As established in the previous section, further work on the theoretical understanding of BPM in general and service innovation in specific is still needed. While BPM and related concepts such as TQM or Business Process Reengineering are well understood from a practical perspective, they are often studied without proper theoretical foundations. However, a theoretical framework that helps understanding BPM would also lever the applicability of related methods and tools for support. In this SpringerBrief, this initial problem will be backed up with the help of a structured literature review.

In order to tackle this gap, the concept of BPM (and service innovation) has to be conceptualized from a theoretical perspective. Research Question 1 (RQ.1) thus reads as follows:

RQ.1 *How can the concept of business process management be conceptualized from a theoretical perspective?*

RQ.1 will be addressed with the help of theoretical-conceptual work on BPM and service innovation. It will be shown that BPM fits into the dynamic capability framework. The dynamic capability framework is an extension of the resource-based view (RBV) of the firm (Teece et al. 1997). BPM and service innovation can both be understood as process-oriented dynamic capabilities. These are the capabilities for integrating, building, and reconfiguring organizational processes.

This conceptualization of BPM (and service innovation) as a process-oriented dynamic capability has to be tested in empirical applications (Bullinger et al. 2003). RQ.2 thus asks:

RQ.2 *How far is this theoretical conceptualization of process-oriented dynamic capabilities valid when applied to real world phenomena?*

RQ.2 will be addressed with the help of qualitative and quantitative research. In several case studies in four organizations, it will be shown that the developed theoretical framework of process-oriented dynamic capabilities is valid and valuable when studying service innovation or BPM. Two quantitative studies will be used to support these qualitative claims.

Based on these applications of the theoretical conceptualization to real world phenomena and focusing on the service sector, RQ.3 states:

RQ.3 *How can process-oriented dynamic capabilities in the service sector be supported methodologically?*

With RQ.3 the research gap described by Bullinger et al. will be tackled. They argue that "[d]escription methods and model[l]ing tools developed specifically for service engineering [...] are essentially lacking." (Bullinger et al. 2003, pp. 285f.) RQ.3 will be addressed using design-oriented research. The resulting method will be evaluated in a laboratory experiment.

This SpringerBrief is structured in six chapters. It starts with the motivation, objective, and structure of this research (this chapter). Next, the research background (Chap. 2) and the sequential multi-method research approach are presented (Chap. 3). Chapter 4 summarizes the main results with respect to the six sequences of the research approach. Moreover, in Chap. 5, limitations and implications for both theory and practice are discussed. This SpringerBrief ends with a short conclusion of the work (Chap. 6).

# References

Armistead, C., & Machin, S. (1997). Implications of business process management for operations management. *International Journal of Operations and Production Management, 17*(9), 886–898.

Armistead, C., & Machin, S. (1998). Business process management: Implications for productivity in multi-stage service networks. *International Journal of Service Industry Management, 9*(4), 323–336.

Berry, L. L., Shankar, V., Parish, J. T., Cadwallader, S., & Dotzel, T. (2006). Creating new markets through service innovation. *MIT Sloan Management Review, 47*(2), 56–63.

Bitner, M. J., Ostrom, A. L., & Morgan, F. N. (2008). Service blueprinting: A practical technique for service innovation. *California Management Review, 50*(3), 66–95.

Bullinger, H.-J., Fähnrich, K.-P., & Meiren, T. (2003). Service engineering: Methodical development of new service products. *International Journal of Production Economics, 85*(3), 275–287.

Enterprise and Industry Magazine (2011). Service innovation can give Europe a cutting edge. In *European Union Enterprise and Industry Magazine.*

Gartner Inc. (2012). *Amplifying the Enterprise: Insights from the 2012 Gartner CIO Agenda Report.*

Hipp, C., Tether, B. S., & Miles, I. (2000). The incidence and effects of innovation in services: Evidence from Germany. *International Journal of Innovation Management, 4*(4), 417–453.

Katzan, H. (2008). *Service science: Concepts, technology, management.* New York: iUniverse.

Loftus, T. (2013). CIOs: Hardwire to the business. Retrieved January 28, 2013, from http://blogs.wsj.com/cio/2013/01/17/cios-hardwire-to-the-business/

Maglio, P. P., & Spohrer, J. (2007). Fundamentals of service science. *Journal of the Academy of Marketing Science, 36*(1), 18–20.

Maleyeff, J. (2011). Factors impacting innovation in new service offerings. *Journal of Service Science and Management, 4*(2), 111–117.

Melão, N., & Pidd, M. (2000). A conceptual framework for understanding business processes and business process modelling. *Information Systems Journal, 10*(2), 105–129.

Niehaves, B., Plattfaut, R., & Becker, J. (2010). Does your business process management (still) fit the market?—a dynamic capability perspective on BPM strategy development. In *Proceedings of the 16th Americas Conference on Information Systems (AMCIS)*, Lima, Peru.

Pöppelbuß, J., Plattfaut, R., Ortbach, K., Malsbender, A., Voigt, M., Niehaves, B., et al. (2011). Service innovation capability: Proposing a new framework. In *Proceedings of the 3rd International Symposium on Services Science (ISSS) in conjunction with the Federated Conference on Computer Science and Information Systems (FedCSIS)*, Szczecin, Poland.

Pritchard, J.-P., & Armistead, C. (1999). Business process management—lessons from European business. *Business Process Management Journal, 5*(1), 10–32.

PwC (2013). *16th Annual Global CEO Survey: Dealing with disruption, adapting to survive and thrive.*

Rosemann, M., De Bruin, T., & Power, B. (2006). A model to measure business process management maturity and improve performance. In J. Jeston & J. Nelis (Eds.), *Business process management: Practical guidelines to successful implementations* (pp. 299–315). Burlington: Butterworth Heinemann.

Smart, P. A., Maddern, H., & Maull, R. S. (2009). Understanding business process management: Implications for theory and practice. *British Journal of Management, 20*(4), 491–507.

Teece, D. J., Pisano, G., & Shuen, A. (1997). Dynamic capabilities and strategic management. *Strategic Management Journal, 18*(7), 509–533.

Tether, B. S. (2002). The sources and aims of innovation in services: Variety between and within sectors. *Economics of Innovation and New Technology, 12*(6), 481–505.

Zairi, M. (1997). Business process management: A boundaryless approach to modern competitiveness. *Business Process Management Journal, 3*(1), 64–80.

# Chapter 2
# Research Background

## 2.1 Business Process Management

Business Process Management (BPM) is a holistic management approach towards changing an organization's business processes (Armistead and Machin 1997, 1998; Pritchard and Armistead 1999; Rosemann et al. 2006; Zairi 1997). Following Becker and Kahn (2010), business processes can be defined as time-logical sequences of activities that are conducted to work on a process-oriented business object (e.g., an invoice) to achieve corresponding business goals. In turn, BPM refers to changing these sequences of activities. As such, it is a top business and IT priority in organizations and a core topic in IS research. The roots of BPM are twofold (Niehaves et al. 2011): Firstly, BPM is based on the concept of Business Process Reengineering (Peppard and Fitzgerald 1997). Business Process Reengineering emphasizes the radical and revolutionary change of organizations (Davenport and Short 1990; Hammer 1990). This change is often induced by IT innovations. Secondly, BPM is also based on the concept of Total Quality Management (Hung 2006; Zairi and Sinclair 1995), which is a rather incremental and evolutionary approach which aims at continuous improvement of business processes.

Hence, BPM can be defined as an organization's ability to change (e.g., integrate, build, reconfigure, improve, adapt, adjust, refresh, renew, etc.) the organization's business processes. It includes measures for both punctuated (radical) and incremental (evolutionary) change of business processes (Niehaves et al. 2010).

BPM covers both organizational and technical perspectives (Stohr and Zhao 2001; Sun et al. 2006). Gartner (2010) reports that business process improvement was the #1 business priority on CIOs' agendas in 2010. According to McKinsey (2008), the improvement of efficiency and effectiveness of business processes was the top IT priority for 2009. However, organizations still lack BPM capabilities (Gartner Inc. 2012).

BPM capabilities must not necessarily reside in the organization itself (Niehaves et al. 2011). Instead, the organization may source BPM capabilities from market, network, and hierarchy (Powell 1990). Firstly, market refers to economic actions regulated by prices. Organizations can obtain their BPM capabilities on the market by, e.g., hiring external consultants that support or conduct complex process change projects (Niehaves et al. 2011). Secondly, network refers to cooperative partnerships of partners with complementary strengths and common interests (Powell 1990). The partners come together to solve common problems in a trustful and communicative manner. Exemplarily, organizations could work together with their suppliers to improve important business processes. Thirdly, hierarchical sourcing comes out of an employer/employee relation (Powell 1990). This relation is quite stable and forms a reliable work environment. One BPM related example is a firm that uses own employees on BPM-related tasks (Niehaves et al. 2011).

## 2.2  Business Process Management Capability Development

The focus of contemporary BPM research also includes the discussion of BPM capabilitiy development. A shortage of advice on BPM strategy design, BPM adoption, and evolution models exists (Rosemann 2010). Presently, a major issue is how organizations can and should develop their BPM capabilities (Niehaves et al. 2013). Literature provides a prolific discussion of capability assessment and development models in the private (De Bruin and Rosemann 2007; Rosemann et al. 2006) and in the public sector (Zwicker et al. 2010). These BPM capability development models are predominantly maturity models. Maturity models often build upon the Capability Maturity Model (Paulk et al. 1993) or related models. As such, they have the three goals of description, prescription, and comparison (Röglinger et al. 2012; Rosemann et al. 2006). Usually, they have a number of stages through which an organization proceeds when developing BPM capabilities. The highest stage is defined as being the most beneficial. Thus, organizations should follow this prescribed sequential path until the highest stage is achieved. Maturity models often argue that any divergence from the prescribed path should be corrected before moving onwards to the highest stage possible (Fisher 2004). The stages are used to quantify and summarize the evaluation and, thus, make organizations comparable (Rosemann et al. 2006). The maturity models define several capability areas, factors, action fields, or levers of change for each stage.

## 2.3  Service Innovation

Services are time-perishable intangible experiences performed by a service provider for a client (Spohrer and Maglio 2008). The customer owns or controls certain inputs that the service provider transforms according to a mutual agreement (Spohrer and Maglio 2008; Spohrer et al. 2007). Services are commonly defined by multiple characteristics that distinguish them from manufactured goods. Services are intangible and perishable. They cannot be stored or produced on stock

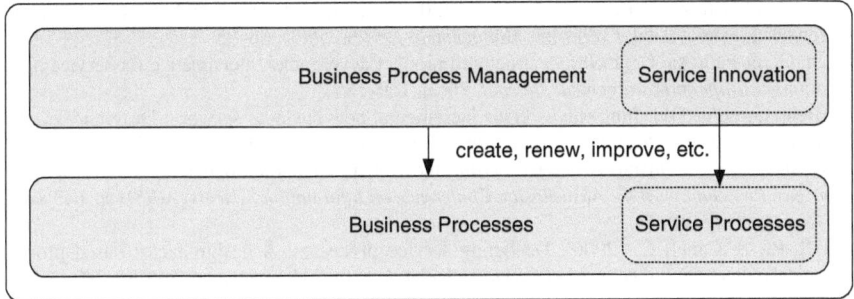

**Fig. 2.1**  BPM and service innovation

(Das and Canel 2006; Katzan 2008). Service provision and consumption cannot be seperated and happen simultaneously (Das and Canel 2006). Moreover, the provision of a service differs in nature and quality from time to time as both service provider and service customer bring different inputs into the service provision process (Katzan 2008). Most importantly, a distinctive characteristic of services is their process nature (Bitner et al. 2008; Katzan 2008).

Service innovation refers to the organizational capabilities for the creation of new services and the incremental change of existing ones (Den Hertog et al. 2010; Pöppelbuß et al. 2011). As such, service innovation comprises measures of incremental and radical change (Armistead and Machin 1997; de Brentani 2001; Droege et al. 2009; Oke 2007). Service innovation is at least different if not more complex than the development of new (manufactured) products (Bitran and Pedrosa 1998; Den Hertog et al. 2010; Johne and Storey 1998; Stevens and Dimitriadis 2005). Exemplarily, changes to the value proposition offered to the customer and changes to the service provision process are mutually interdependent and intertwined (Droege et al. 2009).

Following the conceptualization of BPM and service innovation, it becomes clear that both are related to one another. In fact, service innovation can be understood as those organizational abilities that refer to the change and creation of service processes while BPM covers the abilities for general process change. Thus, service innovation can be seen as a special case of BPM (Fig. 2.1).

## References

Armistead, C., & Machin, S. (1998). Business process management: Implications for productivity in multi-stage service networks. *International Journal of Service Industry Management, 9*(4), 323–336.

Armistead, C., & Machin, S. (1997). Implications of business process management for operations management. *International Journal of Operations & Production Management, 17*(9), 886–898.

Becker, J., & Kahn, D. (2010). The process in focus. In J. Becker, M. Kugeler, & M. Rosemann (Eds.), *Process management* (2nd ed., pp. 3–14). Berlin/Heidelberg: Springer.

Bitner, M. J., Ostrom, A. L., & Morgan, F. N. (2008). Service blueprinting: A practical technique for service innovation. *California Management Review, 50*(3), 66–95.

Bitran, G., & Pedrosa, L. (1998). A structured product development perspective for service operations. *European Management Journal, 16*(2), 169–189.

De Brentani, U. (2001). Innovative versus incremental new business services: Different keys for achieving success. *Journal of Product Innovation Management, 18*(3), 169–187.

De Bruin, T., & Rosemann, M. (2007). Using the Delphi Technique to Identify BPM Capability Areas. *Proceedings of the Australasian Conference on Information Systems (ACIS)* (pp. 643–653). Toowoomba, Australia.

Das, S. R., & Canel, C. (2006). Designing service processes: A design factor based process model. *International Journal of Services, Technology and Management, 7*(1), 85–107.

Davenport, T. H., & Short, J. E. (1990). The new industrial engineering: information technology and business process redesign. *Sloan Management Review, 31*(4), 11–27.

Droege, H., Hildebrand, D., & Forcada, M. A. H. (2009). Innovation in services: Present findings, and future pathways. *International Journal of Service Industry Management, 20*(2), 131–155.

Fisher, D. M. (2004). The business process maturity model: A practical approach for identifying opportunities for optimization. *Business Process Trends, 9*(4).

Gartner Inc. (2012). *Amplifying the Enterprise: Insights from the 2012 Gartner CIO Agenda Report.*

Gartner Inc. (2010). *Leading in Times of Transition: The 2010 CIO Agenda*, Egham, UK.

Hammer, M. (1990). Reengineering work: Don't automate, obliterate. *Harvard Business Review, 68*(4), 104–122.

Den Hertog, P., Van Der Aa, W., & De Jong, M. W. (2010). Capabilities for managing service innovation: Towards a conceptual framework. *Journal of Service Management, 21*(4), 490–514.

Hung, R. (2006). Business process management as competitive advantage: A review and empirical study. *Total Quality Management & Business Excellence, 17*(1), 21–40.

Johne, A., & Storey, C. (1998). New service development: A review of the literature and annotated bibliography. *European Journal of Marketing, 32*(3–4), 184–251.

Katzan, H. (2008). *Service science: Concepts, technology, management.* New York: iUniverse.

Robert, R., & Sikes, J. (2008). McKinsey global survey results: It's unmet potential. *McKinsey Quarterly 17*(4), 1–9.

Niehaves, B., Plattfaut, R., & Becker, J. (2013). Business process management capabilities in local governments: A multi-method study. *Government Information Quarterly (accepted for publication)*.

Niehaves, B., Plattfaut, R., & Becker, J. (2010). Does your business process management (still) fit the market?—A dynamic capability perspective on bpm strategy development. *Proceedings of the 16th Americas Conference on Information Systems (AMCIS)*, Lima, Peru.

Niehaves, B., Plattfaut, R., Budde, M., & Becker, J. (2011). Business process governance: A qualitative case study at production. *Proceedings of the 17th Americas Conference on Information Systems (AMCIS)*, Detroit, USA.

Oke, A. (2007). Innovation types and innovation management practices in service companies. *International Journal of Operations & Production Management, 27*(6), 564–587.

Paulk, M. C., Curtis, B., Chrissis, M. B., & Weber, C. V. (1993). *Capability maturity model for software, version 1.1*, Software Engineering Institute, Carnegie Mellon University.

Peppard, J. W., & Fitzgerald, D. (1997). The transfer of culturally-grounded management techniques: The case of business reengineering in Germany. *European Management Journal, 15*(4), 446–460.

Pöppelbuß, J., Plattfaut, R., Ortbach, K., Malsbender, A., Voigt, M., Niehaves, B., et al. (2011). Service innovation capability: Proposing a new framework. *Proceedings of the 3rd International Symposium on Services Science (ISSS) in conjunction with the Federated Conference on Computer Science and Information Systems (FedCSIS)*, Szczecin, Poland.

Powell, W. W. (1990). Neither market nor hierarchy: Network forms of organization. *Research in Organizational Behavior, 12*(1), 295–336.

Pritchard, J.-P., & Armistead, C. (1999). Business process management—lessons from European business. *Business Process Management Journal, 5*(1), 10–32.

Röglinger, M., Pöppelbuß, J., & Becker, J. (2012). Maturity models in business process management. *Business Process Management Journal, 18*(2), 328–349.

Rosemann, M., De Bruin, T., & Power, B. (2006). A model to measure business process management maturity and improve performance. In J. Jeston & J. Nelis (Eds.), *Business process management: Practical guidelines to successful implementations* (pp. 299–315). Burlington, USA: Butterworth Heinemann.

Rosemann, M. (2010). The service portfolio of a bpm center of excellence. In: J. vom Brocke & M. Rosemann (Eds.), *Handbook on Business Process Management 2* (pp. 267–284). Berlin/Heidelberg: Springer.

Spohrer, J. C., Maglio, P. P., Bailey, J., & Gruhl, D. (2007). Steps towards a science of service systems. *Computer, 40*(1), 71–77.

Spohrer, J. C., & Maglio, P. P. (2008). The emergence of service science: Toward systematic service innovations to accelerate co-creation of value. *Production and Operations Management, 17*(3), 238–246.

Stevens, E., & Dimitriadis, S. (2005). Managing the new service development process: Towards a systemic model. *European Journal of Marketing, 39*(1–2), 175–198.

Stohr, E. A., & Zhao, J. L. (2001). Workflow automation: Overview and research issues. *Information Systems Frontiers, 3*(3), 281–296.

Sun, S. X., Zhao, J. L., Nunamaker, J. F., & Sheng, O. R. L. (2006). Formulating the data-flow perspective for business process management. *Information Systems Research, 17*(4), 374–391.

Zairi, M., & Sinclair, D. (1995). Business process re-engineering and process management: A survey of current practice and future trends in integrated management. *Management Decision, 33*(3), 3–16.

Zairi, M. (1997). Business process management: A boundaryless approach to modern competitiveness. *Business Process Management Journal, 3*(1), 64–80.

Zwicker, J., Fettke, P., & Loos, P. (2010). Business process maturity in public administrations. In J. vom Brocke & M. Rosemann (Eds.), *Handbook on Business Process Management 2* (pp. 369–400). Berlin/Heidelberg: Springer.

# Chapter 3
# Research Approach

## 3.1 Overview

In order to answer the introduced research questions, a multi-method research approach was employed (Creswell 2003). Multi-method research is increasingly used and accepted in social sciences (Bryman and Bell 2011) and is considered as being valuable for IS research for three main reasons. Firstly, Mingers argues that the world itself is multi-dimensional and hence too complex to be captured by only one single research method. "Multi-method research is necessary to deal effectively with the full richness of the real world." (Mingers 2001, p. 243) Secondly, research is rather a process than a discrete event. This process can be divided into the four phases of appreciation, analysis, assessment, and action (Mingers 2001, 2003). Each of these phases will need different research methods. Lastly, several authors give rise to the argument that multi-method research has advantages with regards to reliability and robustness of the findings (Kaplan and Duchon 1988; Niehaves 2010).

The research approach applies multiple methods in a sequential way. Results from earlier sequences feed into later ones (Mingers 2001). Such a sequential multi-method research approach is established in IS research. One example of this approach is given by Gable (1994). He illustrates the specific benefits of integrating case study research with survey research in a sequential manner (Gable 1994). According to his research, case studies help in developing a conceptual model that can be tested using survey research. Furthermore, he argues that the case studies can be useful to develop a close relationship with organizations. This relationship can be used for pilot testing of the research model and for interpreting the quantitative findings later on (Gable 1994). Another example is given by Kaplan and Duchon (1988). They combine quantitative and qualitative research methods and argue that such a combination introduces both context and testability into the research (Kaplan and Duchon 1988).

The sequential multi-method research approach is depicted in Table 3.1. It consists of the following six sequences. Firstly, in order to appreciate the problem

R. Plattfaut, *Process-Oriented Dynamic Capabilities*, SpringerBriefs in Information Systems, DOI: 10.1007/978-3-319-03251-1_3, © The Author(s) 2014

**Table 3.1** Research approach

| # | RQ | Research method | Data | Publications |
|---|-----|----------------|------|-------------|
| 1 | | Literature review (vom Brocke et al. 2009; Webster and Watson 2002) | Prior literature | (Niehaves and Plattfaut 2011) |
| 2 | RQ.1 | Conceptual-theoretical work supported by first case study results (Yin 2003) | Prior literature, case studies PUBLIC and PHONESERV | (Niehaves et al. 2010; Ortbach et al. 2012) |
| 3 | RQ.2 | Case study research (Yin 2003) | Case studies OFFICE, IT–CONSULT, PUBLIC | (Niehaves et al. 2011a, b; Niehaves et al. 2013; Plattfaut et al. 2012; Plattfaut 2012) |
| 4 | RQ.2 | Quantitative survey research (Ringle et al. 2012; Weiber and Mühlhaus 2010) | Quantitative data sets local administrations and service firms | (Niehaves et al. 2012; Plattfaut et al. 2013a, b) |
| 5 | RQ.3 | Design-oriented research (Hevner et al. 2004; March and Smith 1995) | Prior results and insights from case studies | (Becker et al. 2013; Voigt et al. 2013, b) |
| 6 | RQ.3 | Laboratory experiment (Levy and Ellis 2011) | Quantitative and qualitative data from experiments with practitioners and students | (Voigt et al. 2013c) |

area and confirm the existence of the research gaps, a thorough literature review was conducted. Secondly, to address RQ.1, a theoretical framework to understand BPM and service innovation was developed in theoretical-conceptual work. This work was supported by first case study results. Thirdly, RQ.2 was addressed using case study research. Case study research was employed to refine the theoretical understanding and to apply it in different real-world settings. Both case study partners and results also helped to develop and pilot test the conceptual research models used for, fourthly, survey research as suggested by Gable (1994). Survey research helps addressing RQ.2, too. Survey research was used to evaluate the theoretical framework and the derived research models which incorporated service innovation, collaboration, IT support, and their corresponding influence on service provision success. In order to answer RQ.3, two more sequences that correspond to Mingers' action phase (2001, 2003) were needed: Fifthly, based on the results of the quantitative survey, a method to support process-oriented service innovation was developed using design-oriented research. Lastly, this method for process-oriented service innovation was evaluated using an experiment in a laboratory setting.

In the subsequent sections, the five research methods employed in the six sequences of the multi-method research approach (literature review, case study research, quantitative survey research, design-oriented research, and laboratory experiment) will be explained briefly.


## 3.2 Literature Review

One substantial step of any research endeavor is the review of prior work in the specific area of study (Baker 2000; vom Brocke et al. 2009). By uncovering the relevant sources, the literature review makes an important contribution to both relevance and rigor of the research endeavor (vom Brocke et al. 2009). On the one hand, the reinvestigation of what is already known is avoided which improves relevance (Baker 2000; Bryman and Bell 2011; Creswell 2003). On the other hand, the effective use of the knowledge base helps improving scientific rigor (Hevner et al. 2004). Thus, it is clear that literature reviews play a central role in scholarship in general (Cooper 1988) and in IS research in specific (vom Brocke et al. 2009; Levy and Ellis 2006; Webster and Watson 2002).

The literature review (Niehaves and Plattfaut 2011) was conducted in a systematic way which followed the guidelines proposed by vom Brocke et al. (2009). Their guidelines are in turn based on Webster and Watson (2002). At first, the major outlets of the field (i.e., the Association for Information Systems' (AIS) Senior Scholars' Basket of Journals and the proceedings of the International Conference of Information Systems) as well as specialized outlets (i.e., the Business Process Management Journal and the proceedings of the International Conference on Business Process Management) were searched using an appropriate search term. This search was conducted in title, abstract, and keywords of the articles. Afterwards, the search was extended with a database search in ISI Web of Knowledge's Web of Science, which, at the time of search, covered more than 11,000 different journals. Again, the search term was used to search title, abstract, and keywords. Lastly, a backward search was conducted. In this backward search, the reference lists of the articles identified were scanned for further relevant articles. After each of the three steps, the identified articles were scanned for relevancy to the topic. The resulting list of articles consists of 37 articles from various outlets. They were analyzed with the help of a concept matrix (Webster and Watson 2002) derived from literature.


## 3.3 Case Study Research

Case study research is said to be the most common qualitative research method used in IS research (Myers 2008). Numerous definitions of case study research exist. In accordance with Myers (2012), the definition of Yin (2003) was used: "A case study is an empirical enquiry that investigates a contemporary phenomenon within its real-life context, especially when the boundaries between phenomenon and context are not clearly evident." (Yin 2003, p. 13) Case study research is especially suitable when "how" or "why" questions are being asked (Yin 2003), which is the case for the research questions presented in Sect. 1.2. In general, case study researchers examine a phenomenon in the corresponding natural setting with as little interference as possible (Oates 2006).

In this SpringerBrief, results from seven in-depth case studies in four organizations are analyzed (Niehaves et al. 2010, 2011a, b, 2013; Ortbach et al. 2012; Plattfaut et al. 2012; Plattfaut 2012). These organizations stem from different industries, mostly in the service sector, and are named PUBLIC (public services), PHONESERV (telecommunication services), OFFICE (office supplies), and IT-CONSULT (IT-consulting) for reasons of anonymity. A brief description of all four organizations and the corresponding case settings is given in the following and in Table 3.2.

PUBLIC is a local government in North-Rhine-Westphalia. It is among the largest public authorities in Germany. Due to a large budget deficit of the municipality, the financial situation of PUBLIC is tight. Thus, PUBLIC follows the two goals of cost-cutting and efficiency-improvement. Moreover, PUBLIC faces new challenges, such as E-Government or the EU service directive, which are environmental drivers for process and service innovation. From an organizational perspective, responsibilities for process innovation are in the organization department. However, as most public administrations PUBLIC cannot be considered very innovative. The case study PUBLIC was used in three publications (Niehaves et al. 2010, 2013; Plattfaut 2012).

PHONESERV is among the five largest telecommunication companies in Germany. It provides a variety of communication services including digital subscriber line (DSL) and very-high-bit-rate digital subscriber line (VDSL) as well as (mobile) telephony and internet protocol television (IPTV) to around 2.3 Million customers in the DSL market and more than 630,000 customers in the mobile communication market. PHONESERV pursues process-oriented service innovation with the help of their BPM department which serves as a center of excellence. The case study PHONESERV was analyzed in one publication (Ortbach et al. 2012).

OFFICE is a medium-sized production company which operates for over 70 years in the paper, office supplies, and stationary industry. In this market, office is one of the largest companies in Germany. In addition to the production locations in Germany and Poland, OFFICE has sales organizations in more than 60 locations around the world. At the time of data collection, OFFICE increasingly tried to improve the service portfolio. However, service innovation often failed. From a process perspective, processes were often seen as belonging to the realm of quality management. In this setting, no real process innovations were conducted. This is also reflected in the organizational structure which is still very function-oriented. The case study OFFICE was used in two publications (Niehaves et al. 2011a, b).

IT-CONSULT is a medium sized IT-consultancy that was founded around the end of the 1990s. At the moment of data collection, it employed about 50

**Table 3.2** Case settings

| Company | PUBLIC | PHONESERV | OFFICE | IT-CONSULT |
|---|---|---|---|---|
| Industry | Local administration | Telecommunication | Office supplies | IT-consulting |
| Annual turnover | – | 1.2 Billion € | 110 Million € | >50 Million € |
| Number of employees | >6,000 | 2,300 | 750 | 46 |
| Main period of data collection | 06/2009–01/2010 | 11/2008–01/2009 | 10/2008–12/2008 and 10/2009–12/2009 | 11/2010 |
| Number of interviews | 12 | 9 | 21 | 4 |
| Positions of interviewees | Head and middle managers of organization and HR development, employees in organization and HR development, IT controller, financial manager, employee in branch office, deputy head official, quality manager, unit manager | Head and middle managers of strategic process management, head of cost management, head of operations (sales & order), head of operations (billing and cancellation), head of service controlling, head of BPM, employee in quality management, head of IT | Heads and middle managers of material management, product development, product management, quality management, IT and organization, purchasing and incoming goods, back office | Partners, project manager |

consultants and developers. IT-CONSULT supports organizations in the introduction of software applications, often standardized enterprise resource planning (ERP) systems. IT-CONSULT is specialized in SAP ERP implementation projects and focuses on three customer segments: public sector organizations (e.g., municipalities), utilities (e.g., electricity suppliers), and financial services (e.g., insurances and banks). The case study IT-CONSULT was used in one publication (Plattfaut et al. 2012).

In all four cases, several sources of evidence were used. These did not only cover interviews as presented in Table 3.2 but also, e.g., direct observations, publications, process models, or supplementary material. However, the interviews formed the primary source of evidence. Typically, they lasted between 30 min and 2 h. All interviews were transcribed.

## 3.4 Quantitative Survey Research

Quantitative survey research generally provides a quantitative description of attitudes, perceptions, or opinions of a population. This description is derived by studying a sample of a specific population and generalizing from the sample to that larger population (Creswell 2003; Groves et al. 2004; Pinsonneault and Kraemer 1993; Recker 2013). Quantitative survey research is often used to test theoretical assumptions in terms of research models (Weiber and Mühlhaus 2010). Often, the hypotheses and research models are transferred to structural equations and corresponding structural equation models (Gefen et al. 2011; Henseler et al. 2009; Ringle et al. 2012; Weiber and Mühlhaus 2010). Structural equation modeling (SEM) methods can be considered to be among the most important multivariate analysis methods in contemporary IS research (Gefen et al. 2011; Ringle et al. 2012).

In the quantitative studies for this SpringerBrief, the data was analyzed using partial least squares (PLS) SEM (PLS-SEM, Ringle et al. 2012). The analyses were supported by the software tool SmartPLS 2.0 M3 (Ringle et al. 2005). A brief description of the two different data sets used for the quantitative survey research is given in the following and in Table 3.3.

The first data set of local administrations was collected in 2008. It covers 358 cases of German and 180 cases of Japanese local administrations. As such, it covers about 3 % of all German and 10 % of all Japanese local administrations. In each municipality one government official was identified who answered questions with regards to BPM, process innovation, BPM networks, etc. The questions used here were part of a larger questionnaire (Niehaves 2008). In Germany, the questionnaire was sent to local administrations via e-mail and could be answered online. In Japan, data collection was conducted paper-based. In both cases, the questionnaire was translated into the corresponding language. After a first descriptive analysis of the German parts of the data set (Niehaves et al. 2013), the data set was further analyzed (Niehaves et al. 2012).

**Table 3.3** Quantitative data sets

| Data set | Local administrations | Service firms |
|---|---|---|
| Industry | Local administration | Service sector in general, concentration on SME |
| Geographic distribution | Germany, Japan | Germany |
| Period of data collection | 2008 | 2012 |
| Valid answers | n = 538 | n = 600 (including n = 100 from first round) |
| Respondents | Local government officials | Representatives for service innovation |

The second data set of service firms was collected in 2012. It covers 600 cases of German service organizations. With the help of a market research firm, 2,561 service organizations were contacted by telephone. The first goal was to identify a representative for service innovation. Then, this representative was asked to answer the questions of the questionnaire. As the identification of a representative for service innovation can be quite difficult in larger organizations, only small and medium-sized enterprises (SMEs) were contacted. Here, a German definition of SME was used: Organizations should have less than 500 employees and an annual turn-over of below 50 Million Euros (IfM_Bonn 2012). In a first round, the answers of 100 service firms were collected and used to test an initial research model (Plattfaut et al. 2013a). As there were no issues with regards to validity of the research model, further data was collected in a second round. The joint sample of both phases consists of 600 SMEs out of the German service sector (response rate of 23.4 %). The respondents were top managers (22 %), middle managers (71 %), or had other positions (7 %). The service firms came from different sub-sectors including IT-services (38 %), financial services (23 %), and public services (16 %). This data set was also analyzed in full (Plattfaut et al. 2013b).

## 3.5 Design-Oriented Research

Design-oriented research is about the creation of innovative artifacts, such as constructs, models, methods, and technological instantiations (March and Smith 1995), that are useful for dealing with human and organizational challenges (Hevner et al. 2004). Although not new (Baskerville 2008), the importance of design-oriented research for the IS field appears to be growing (Baskerville 2008; Gregor and Jones 2007; Hevner et al. 2004; Kuechler and Vaishnavi 2008, 2012; Peffers et al. 2007). However, a commonly accepted reference research process is still missing (Winter and Baskerville 2010). In their seminal work, March and Smith's (1995) argue that design science research consists of two main activities (or phases): build and evaluate. Using this basic differentiation, the design-oriented research presented in this SpringerBrief can be structured into an iterative cycle of these two phases.

The artifact designed is a method to create process-oriented service innovations and builds upon prior work on business model innovation (Becker et al. 2013; Voigt et al. 2013a). The method was initially created (build 1), tested with the help of students (evaluate 1), modified according to their feedback (build 2), tested with the help of professionals from three service-oriented companies (evaluate 2), and modified again according to their feedback (build 3). Moreover, a further, more rigor evaluation of the method using a laboratory experiment (Sect. 3.6) was conducted, too (Voigt et al. 2013c).

Moreover, the method was implemented in a software prototype (Becker et al. 2013; Voigt et al. 2013b). The implementation team consisted of 21 members (students and research assistants). This prototype is a rich internet application that builds upon the Ruby on Rails framework and uses Asynchronous JavaScript and XML.

## 3.6 Laboratory Experiments

Experiments are used to measure the influence of independent variables (treatment) on several dependent variables (Benbasat et al. 1987; Creswell 2003; Levy and Ellis 2011). Typically, two main types of experiments are differentiated: Lab(oratory) experiments and field experiments (Benbasat et al. 1987; Levy and Ellis 2011; Mingers 2003; Nunamaker et al. 1996). Firstly, lab experiments are the true form of experiments in which the researcher has a great amount of control over the study. The researcher is able to select the participants and (often) assigns them randomly into different study groups. As such, the environment is controlled (Benbasat et al. 1987). Typically, the effect of a specific treatment on several dependent variables is measured (Levy and Ellis 2011). Secondly, field experiments (also named in situ or quasi-experiments) are experiments in which the control of the researcher is limited. Often, participant selection and assignment to different study groups is not possible but given by the situation (Levy and Ellis 2011). Thus, the setting can be considered to be more natural (Benbasat et al. 1987). However, other uncontrolled variables might influence the results. This conflict between the naturalness or richness of worldly realism and the tightness of control is considered to be a fundamental tradeoff that cannot be resolved (Mason 1989). In general, experiments are considered valid for evaluating the results of design-oriented research (Venable et al. 2012).

For this publication, an experiment was conducted to evaluate the created method for process-oriented service innovation (Voigt et al. 2013c). To prevent external uncontrolled influences, the experiment took place in a laboratory setting. The experiment was a group experiment in order to lever the relevance for collaborative service innovations. 81 subjects participated in the experiment (21 female and 60 male). All participants had a business background, either because they were enrolled in corresponding university programs (41 undergraduate and 28 graduate students) or because they were professionals from related industries (12 participants). Overall, the vast majority had working experience, e.g., through regular jobs, internships, or student jobs. The participants were organized in groups of three, while controlling for the average creative potential of the groups using the Creative Personality Scale (Gough 1979). The group size of three was chosen as it allows for the largest number of groups with the given number of subjects (Fjermestad and Hiltz 1998). Group members were trained with one specific method for business model innovation: Either a reference method that is highly accepted in practice (the Business Model Canvas (BMC) by Osterwalder and Pigneur 2010) or the designed artifact (see Sect. 3.5). Afterwards, each group had to create a business model based on the same given real-life business idea. Next, their satisfaction with the corresponding method with regards to several variables was measured using a quantitative questionnaire. Moreover, the results (the created business models) were evaluated by an expert. Thus, the experiment followed an alternative treatment post-test-only with random assignment design (Creswell 2003).

# References

Baker, M. J. (2000). Writing a literature review. *The Marketing Review, 1*(2), 219–247.

Baskerville, R. (2008). What design science is not. *European Journal of Information Systems, 17*(5), 441–443.

Becker, J., Malsbender, A., Ortbach, K., Plattfaut, R., Voigt, M., Höhenberger, S., et al. (2013). Business Modeling-Geschäftsmodelle prozessorientiert und kollaborativ entwickeln, *Zeitschrift Führung + Organisation 82*(2), pp. 137–145.

Benbasat, I., Goldstein, D. K., & Mead, M. (1987). The case research strategy in studies of information systems. *MIS Quarterly, 11*(3), 369–386.

Bryman, A., & Bell, E. (2011). *Business research methods* (3rd ed.). Oxford: Oxford University Press.

Cooper, H. M. (1988). Organizing knowledge syntheses: A taxonomy of literature reviews. *Knowledge in Society, 1*(1), 104–126.

Creswell, J. C. (2003). *Research design: Qualitative, quantitative, and mixed methods approaches* (2nd ed.). Thousand oaks: Sage Publications.

Fjermestad, J., & Hiltz, S. R. (1998). An assessment of group support systems experimental research: Methodology and results. *Journal of Management Information Systems, 15*(3), 7–149.

Gable, G. G. (1994). Integrating case study and survey research methods: An example in information systems. *European Journal of Information Systems, 3*(2), 112–126.

Gefen, D., Rigdon, E. E., & Straub, D. (2011). Editor's comments—an update and extension to SEM guidelines for administrative and social science research. *MIS Quarterly 35*(2), 3–14.

Gough, H. G. (1979). A creative personality scale for the adjective check list. *Journal of Personality and Social Psychology, 37*(8), 1398–1405.

Gregor, S., & Jones, D. (2007). The anatomy of a design theory. *Journal of the Association for Information Systems (AIS), 8*(5), 312–335.

Groves, R. M., Fowler, F. J., Couper, M. P., Lepkowski, J. M., Singer, E., & Tourangeau, R. (2004). *Survey methodology.* Hoboken: John Wiley & Sons.

Henseler, J., Ringle, C. M., & Sinkovics, R. R. (2009). The use of partial least squares path modeling in international marketing. *Advances in International Marketing, 20*, 277–319.

Hevner, A. R., March, S. T., Park, J., & Ram, S. (2004). Design science in information systems research. *MIS Quarterly, 28*(1), 75–105.

IfM_Bonn (2012). KMU-Definition des IfM Bonn. Retrieved 2013-02-01, from http://www.ifm-bonn.org/index.php?id=89.

Kaplan, B., & Duchon, D. (1988). Combining qualitative and quantitative methods in information systems research: A case study. *MIS Quarterly, 12*(4), 571–586.

Kuechler, B., & Vaishnavi, V. (2008). On theory development in design science research: Anatomy of a research project. *European Journal of Information Systems, 17*(5), 489–504.

Kuechler, B., & Vaishnavi, V. (2012). Characterizing design science theories by level of constraint on design decisions, In K. Peffers, M. Rothenberger and B. Kuechler (eds.) *Proceedings of the 7th International Conference on Design Science Research in Information Systems and Technology (DESRIST)* (pp. 345–353), Las Vegas, USA.

Levy, Y., & Ellis, T. J. (2006). A systems approach to conduct an effective literature review in support of information systems research. *Informing Science, 9*, 181–212.

Levy, Y., & Ellis, T. J. (2011). A guide for novice researchers on experimental and quasi-experimental studies in information systems research. *Interdisciplinary Journal of Information, Knowledge, and Management, 6*, 151–161.

March, S. T., & Smith, G. F. (1995). Design and natural science research on information technology. *Decision Support Systems, 15*(4), 251–266.

Mason, R. O. (1989). MIS Experiments: A Pragmatic Perspective. In I. Benbasat (Ed.), *The information systems research challenge: experimental research methods* (pp. 3–20). Boston: Harvard Business Press.

Mingers, J. (2001). Combining IS research methods: Towards a pluralist methodology. *Information Systems Research, 12*(3), 240–259.

Mingers, J. (2003). The paucity of multimethod research: A review of the information systems literature. *Information Systems Journal, 13*(3), 233–249.

Myers, M. D. (2008). Qualitative research in information systems. Retrieved 2008-10-10, from http://www.qual.auckland.ac.nz/.

Niehaves, B. (2008). *Verwaltungsreform in Deutschland und Japan—Kooperative Kommunale Reformpolitik im Vergleich.* Dissertation. Fachgebiet Politikwissenschaften: Westfälische Wilhelms-Universität Münster.

Niehaves, B. (2010). *Business process governance.* Habilitation. Wirtschaftswissenschaftliche Fakultät: Westfälische Wilhelms-Universität Münster.

Niehaves, B., & Plattfaut, R. (2011). Collaborative business process management: Status Quo and Quo Vadis. *Business Process Management Journal, 17*(3), 384–402.

Niehaves, B., Plattfaut, R., & Becker, J. (2010). *Does your business process management (Still) fit the market?—a dynamic capability perspective on BPM strategy developmen. In Proceedings of the 16th Americas Conference on Information Systems (AMCIS).* Peru: Lima.

Niehaves, B., Plattfaut, R., Budde, M., & Becker, J. (2011a). Business process governance: A qualitative case study at production. *Proceedings of the 17th Americas Conference on Information Systems (AMCIS)*, Detroit, USA.

Niehaves, B., Plattfaut, R., & Sarker, S. (2011b). Understanding dynamic is capabilities for effective process change: A theoretical framework and an empirical application. *Proceedings of the 32nd International Conference on Information Systems (ICIS)*, Shanghai, China.

Niehaves, B., Plattfaut, R., & Becker, J. (2012). Business process governance: A comparative study of Germany and Japan. *Business Process Management Journal, 18*(2), 347–371.

Niehaves, B., Plattfaut, R., & Becker, J. (2013). *Business process management capabilities in local governments: A multi-method study.* Government: Information Quarterly (accepted for publication).

Nunamaker, J. F., Briggs, R. O., Mittleman, D. D., Vogel, D. R., & Balthazard, P. A. (1996). Lessons from a dozen years of group support systems research: A discussion of lab and field findings. *Journal of Management Information Systems, 13*(3), 163–207.

Oates, B. J. (2006). *Researching information systems and computing.* Thousand oaks: Sage Publications.

Ortbach, K., Plattfaut, R., Pöppelbuß, J., & Niehaves, B. (2012). A dynamic capability-based framework for business process management: theorizing and empirical application. *Proceedings of the 45th Hawaii International Conference on System Sciences (HICSS)*, Maui, USA.

Osterwalder, A., & Pigneur, Y. (2010). *Business model generation*. New Jersey: Wiley.

Peffers, K., Tuunanen, T., Rothenberger, M. A., & Chatterjee, S. (2007). A design science research methodology for information systems research. *Journal of Management Information Systems, 24*(3), 45–77.

Pinsonneault, A., & Kraemer, K. L. (1993). Survey research methodology in management information systems: An assessment. *Journal of Management Information Systems, 10*(2), 75–105.

Plattfaut, R. (2012). Diskontinuierliche Erwerbsbiografien und alternde Belegschaften als Herausforderung für das Management von Prozessen in der Verwaltung. *Verwaltung & Management, 18*(4), 218–222.

Plattfaut, R., Niehaves, B., & Becker, J. (2012). Capabilities for service innovation: A qualitative case study in the consulting industry. In *Proceedings of the 16th Pacific Asia Conference on Information Systems (PACIS)*, Ho Chi Minh City, Vietnam.

Plattfaut, R., Niehaves, B., Voigt, M., Malsbender, A., Ortbach, K., & Pöppelbuß, J. (2013a). IT and Collaboration in Service Innovation: A Dynamic Capability Perspective. In *Proceedings of the 21st European Conference for Information Systems (ECIS)*, Utrecht, Netherlands.

Plattfaut, R., Niehaves, B., Voigt, M., Malsbender, A., Ortbach, K., & Pöppelbuß, J. (2013b). *What makes service innovation successful? A dynamic capability perspective*, unpublished manuscript.

Recker, J. (2013). *Scientific Research in information systems—a beginner's guide*. Berlin: Springer.

Ringle, C. M., Wende, S., & Will, S. (2005). SmartPLS 2.0 (M3) beta. Retrieved 2011-11-07, from http://www.smartpls.de.

Ringle, C. M., Sarstedt, M., & Straub, D. (2012). Editor's comments—A critical look at the use of PLS-SEM in MIS quarterly. *MIS Quarterly 36*(1), 3–14.

Venable, J., Pries-Heje, J., & Baskerville, R. (2012). A comprehensive framework for evaluation in design science research, In K. Peffers, M. Rothenberger and B. Kuechler (eds.) *Proceedings of the 7th International Conference on Design Science Research in Information Systems and Technology (DESRIST)* (pp. 423–438), Las Vegas, USA.

Voigt, M., Fordey, M., Malsbender, A., Ortbach, K., Plattfaut, R., & Niehaves, B. (2013a). *Business modeling needs process-orientation—framework development and testing*, unpublished manuscript.

Voigt, M., Ortbach, K., Plattfaut, R., & Niehaves, B. (2013b). Developing Creative Business Models—The OctoProz Tool, In *Eighth International Conference on Design Science Research in Information Systems and Technology (DESRIST)*,(pp. 456–462). Helsinki, Finland.

Voigt, M., Plattfaut, R., Ortbach, K., Malsbender, A., & Niehaves, B. (2013c). *Does business modeling benefit from process-thinking? insights from a group experiment*, unpublished manuscript.

Vom Brocke, J., Simons, A., Niehaves, B., Riemer, K., Plattfaut, R., & Cleven, A. (2009) Reconstructing the Giant: On the Importance of Rigour in Documenting the Literature Search Process. In *Proceedings of the 17th European Conference on Information Systems (ECIS)*, Verona, Italy.

Webster, J., & Watson, R. T. (2002). Analyzing the past to prepare for the future: Writing a literature review. *MIS Quarterly 26*(2), 13–23.

Weiber, R., & Mühlhaus, D. (2010). *Strukturgleichungsmodellierung—Eine anwendungsorientierte Einführung in die Kausalanalyse mit Hilfe von AMOS, SmartPLS und SPSS*. Heidelberg: Springer.

Winter, R., & Baskerville, R. (2010). Science of business & information systems engineering. *Business & Information Systems Engineering, 2*(5), 269–270.

Yin, R. K. (2003). *Case study research: Design and methods* (3rd ed.). Thousand oaks: Sage Publications.

# Chapter 4
# Results

## 4.1 Evaluation of the Research Gap

In the exposition (Sect. 4.1), a research gap with regards to the theoretical understanding of BPM and service innovation was outlined. In order to show the existence of this gap and, thus, to prevent an unintended repetition of work that has already been done, a literature review was conducted (Niehaves and Plattfaut 2011). A further goal of this literature review was to analyze in how far current BPM literature has embraced the concept of collaboration. After a structured literature search process (see also Sect. 3.2), 37 relevant articles were identified and analyzed. Three main results of this analysis are of great importance to address the research objectives.

Firstly, results suggest that prior literature focuses equally on the build and work aspects of BPM and processes. In this context, the work aspects (or work system level) refer to the execution of business activities utilizing given organizational and collaborative structures (Alter 2002; Bergman et al. 2002; Lyytinen and Newman 2008). Thus, the work system is about the operational functioning of the organization. These business activities and corresponding structures are designed in a separate build system. The build system has to address issues of uncertainty, complexity, and ambiguity (Lyytinen and Newman 2008; Lyytinen et al. 1996) and is closely related to process innovation and improvement and, thus, to the definition of BPM. Especially this differentiation helped in the further conceptual development of the theoretical understanding (Niehaves and Plattfaut 2011).

Secondly, the literature review showed that several collaboration partners are important for BPM and studied in the literature. These include internal actors such as top management, middle management and employees, or technical specialists. Moreover, external actors such as customers, professional organizations, suppliers, distributors, or consultants are involved in BPM, too (Niehaves and Plattfaut 2011).

R. Plattfaut, *Process-Oriented Dynamic Capabilities*, SpringerBriefs in Information Systems, 23
DOI: 10.1007/978-3-319-03251-1_4, © The Author(s) 2014

Thirdly, out of these and the other results, action fields for future research could be derived. The most important action field refers to a missing theoretical understanding of (collaborative) BPM. It was argued that "several potentially fruitful theory approaches yet appear to be under-developed" (Niehaves and Plattfaut 2011, p. 395) and that it would be especially worth investigating whether BPM fits into the dynamic capability framework (Barreto 2009; Eisenhardt and Martin 2000; Teece 2009; Teece et al. 1997; Winter 2003; Zollo and Winter 2002).

Thus, the literature review underlines the existence of the research gap: So far, more theoretical work on the understanding of (collaborative) BPM is needed.

## 4.2  Conceptual Development of the Theoretical Framework

In order to tackle the research gap with regards to a theoretical understanding of BPM, theoretical-conceptual work supported by first case study research was conducted. As introduced above, especially the consideration of the dynamic capability framework was deemed to be valuable (Niehaves and Plattfaut 2011).

The dynamic capability framework is an extension of the RBV of the firm. RBV was introduced by Wernerfelt (1984) and builds upon prior work (Learned et al. 1969; Penrose 1959). It is widely applied in IS research (Wade and Hulland 2004). According to RBV, organizations can be considered as collections of resources. A resource is defined as "anything which could be thought of as a strength or weakness of a given firm" (Wernerfelt 1984, p. 172).

Resources are either capabilities or assets (Wade and Hulland 2004). Capabilities are the abilities of an organization to perform a coordinated set of tasks for the purpose of achieving a particular end result (Helfat and Peteraf 2003). Thus, capabilities have a strong process perspective. In contrast, assets are anything tangible or intangible the organization can make use of when applying these capabilities (Wade and Hulland 2004), e.g., factories, IT artifacts, or patents. As such, capabilities can be seen as repeatable patterns of actions (Wade and Hulland 2004) or coordinated sets of tasks (Helfat and Peteraf 2003)—or, in short, processes—that utilize assets as inputs (Amit and Schoemaker 1993; Helfat and Peteraf 2003; Niehaves et al. 2010). This understanding is depicted in Fig. 4.1.

Scholars following RBV argue that organizations need resources that fulfill the so-called VRIN conditions in order to achieve a sustained competitive advantage: Resources must be valuable, rare, imperfectly imitable, and non-substitutable (Barney 1991). Resources are valuable to a specific organization when they can be used by that organization in strategies that improve efficiency and effectiveness (Barney 1991). Even valuable resources do not result in competitive advantage if they are not rare (Wade and Hulland 2004). Rarity means that the resource is not simultaneously available to a larger number of organizations (Amit and Schoemaker 1993; Barney 1991; Bowman and Ambrosini 2003; Wade and Hulland 2004). Organizations possessing resources that are valuable and rare

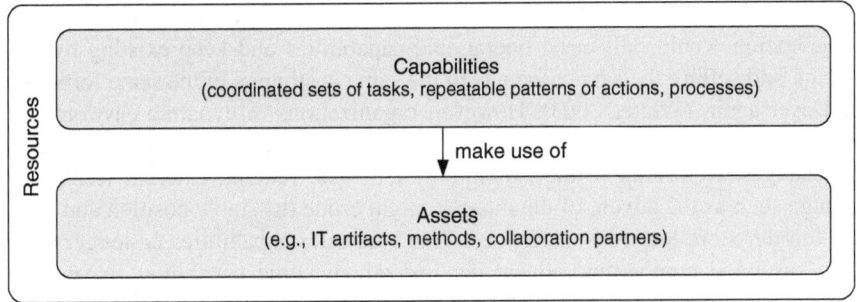

**Fig. 4.1** Capabilities and assets according to the resource-based view

might have certain first-mover advantages (Barney 1991). However, according to RBV, sustained competitive advantage also requires that these resources cannot be imitated (Barney 1991; Wade and Hulland 2004). Moreover, the resources must not only be imperfectly imitable, they should also be non-substitutable: Resources are non-substitutable if only few, if any, resources exist that are strategically equivalent (Amit and Schoemaker 1993; Barney 1991; Wade and Hulland 2004). Barney argues that "two valuable firm resources […] are strategically equivalent when they each can be exploited separately to implement the same strategies" (Barney 1991, p. 111). Exemplarily, a book retailer may have a competitive advantage due to superior sales capabilities supported by several top tier store locations. As especially the store locations are valuable, rare, imperfectly imitable, and non-substitutable, the book retailer is able to sustain this competitive advantage (according to RBV).

In contrast to these arguments, more recent publications argue that organizations should not only concentrate on the VRIN attributes of their resources as this perspective might neglect market dynamics (Bowman and Ambrosini 2003; Daniel and Wilson 2003; Eisenhardt and Martin 2000). Market dynamics may erode a position of competitive advantage, e.g., as new resource substitutes are developed or the value of organizational resources ceases to exist (Collis 1994). Thus, a stable resource configuration does not guarantee sustained competitive advantage in times of dynamic environments (Eisenhardt and Martin 2000). Hence, organizations need specific capabilities that allow them to adapt their resource configuration to environmental changes: Dynamic capabilities (Barreto 2009; Eisenhardt and Martin 2000; Koch 2010; Teece 2009; Teece et al. 1997; Winter 2003; Zollo and Winter 2002). The term dynamic capabilities has been coined by Teece et al. (1997). They define dynamic capabilities as "the firm's ability to integrate, build, and reconfigure internal and external competences to address rapidly changing environments" (Teece et al. 1997, p. 516). In contrast to these dynamic capabilities, operational (or ordinary or zero-level) capabilities are the processes that are executed to "earn a living now" (Winter 2003, p. 992). Operational capabilities can be defined as the organization's ability "to perform a coordinated set of tasks, utilizing organizational assets, for the purpose of the operational functioning of the firm" (Niehaves et al. 2010, p. 3). In a hypothetical static world of no change, an organization would only need operational capabilities and keep existing by producing and selling the same products to the same customers in the same form over and over again (Winter 2003). However, organizations in dynamic environments need dynamic capabilities to adapt their operational capabilities to environmental changes. Returning to the example of the book retailer, external technology change such as the advent of the internet might erode the stable position and make the top-tier store locations superficial. Thus, the sales capabilities no longer result in a sustained competitive advantage. Instead, dynamic capabilities have to be used to reconfigure current capabilities to incorporate online sales channels, too. The differentiation between operational and dynamic capabilities is shown in Fig. 4.2.

BPM can be understood as a dynamic capability (Niehaves et al. 2010). BPM is a holistic management approach that applies measures of both punctuated and incremental change to improve business processes (Armistead and Machin 1997, 1998; Pritchard and Armistead 1999; Rosemann et al. 2006; Zairi 1997). This appears to be in line with the definition of dynamic capabilities, especially considering that restructuring (Zollo and Winter 2002), reengineering (Zollo and Winter 2002), process development (Eisenhardt and Martin 2000), or quality improvement (Zollo and Winter 2002) were already listed as examples for dynamic capabilities. As for the operational capability perspective, business processes can be considered as the coordinated sets of tasks that use organizational assets and have the purpose of the operational functioning of the firm. Thus, business processes are operational capabilities (Niehaves et al. 2010).

The understanding of BPM as a dynamic capability and business processes as the corresponding operational capabilities is supported by other authors, too. In 2010, Trkman argued that "[t]he quest for the achievement of sustainable competitive advantage from BPM can best be described by the DCs' [Dynamic Capabilities'] theory" (Trkman 2010, p. 127). Even more recent, in 2011, Kim et al. coined the term "process-oriented dynamic capabilities" which is used here, too. They define process-oriented dynamic capabilities "as a firm's ability to change (e.g., improve, adapt, adjust, reconfigure, refresh, renew, etc.) a business process

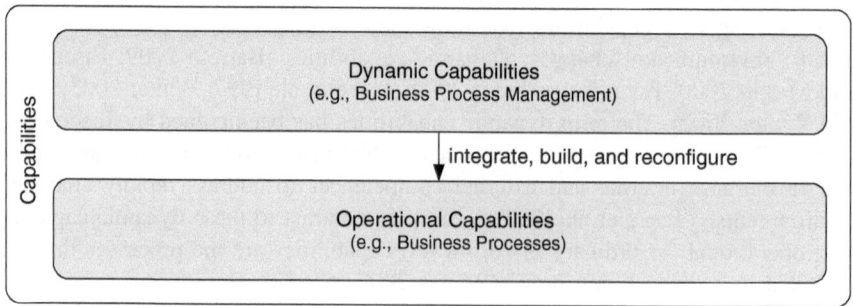

**Fig. 4.2** Differentiation of capabilities according to the dynamic capability framework

better than the competition" (Kim et al. 2011, p. 488). While this definition appears to be appealing, it is not fully in line with the definition of dynamic capabilities in general as it already employs a comparative and evaluative perspective. This argument of being "better than the competition" is not included in the original definition of dynamic capabilities and is thus omitted from the working definition: Process-oriented dynamic capabilities are an organization's abilities to change (e.g., integrate, build, reconfigure, improve, adapt, adjust, refresh, renew, etc.) the organization's processes in order to achieve a fit with the market environment. Thus, process-oriented dynamic capabilities are closely related to the notion of BPM used earlier (Niehaves et al. 2010).

This understanding of BPM as a process-oriented dynamic capability was applied in the case PUBLIC (Niehaves et al. 2010). The results suggest that it is valid and can be used to analyze and explain the status quo in the organization. Evidence for a shift of PUBLIC's environmental dynamics could be found. It could also be shown that PUBLIC lacked the corresponding process-oriented dynamic capabilities to adapt the business processes accordingly. Thus, the case study supports the argument that organizations in dynamic environments need "more" or "better" process-oriented dynamic capabilities to be able to react on environmental changes (Niehaves et al. 2010).

Subsequently, the theoretical framework was further developed (Ortbach et al. 2012). According to Teece (2009), dynamic capabilities in general rely on three classes of activities: Activities for sensing, seizing, and transformation. Firstly, sensing refers to the identification of change needs and opportunities. Secondly, seizing is concerned with the development and selection of solutions. Lastly, transformation refers to the socio-technical implementation of the selected solution in the organization. These three classes of activities appear to be important for the case of process-oriented dynamic capabilities (Ortbach et al. 2012).

The sensing ability is focused on both externally and internally stimulated recognition of possible areas of process change. The externally stimulated identification refers to changing market environments and is in line with the original work of Teece (2009). The focus is on opportunities that result out of changes in the market environment (Bhave 1994), e.g., the introduction of new IT artifacts which can serve to improve business processes or the recognition of new business opportunities which require the introduction of new service processes. However, extending the work of Teece (2009), the internally stimulated recognition of needs for change (Bhave 1994) refers to potential weaknesses and inefficiencies that come up in business processes over time. Both internally and externally stimulated need identification rely on three main activities: (1) scanning, (2) evaluating, and (3) detailing. Firstly, scanning can be defined as the activity of "continuously and deliberatively discovering and surfacing new and useful problems to be solved" (Basadur et al. 2000, p. 60) and serves as a major driver for innovation (DeToro and McCabe 1997; Zairi and Sinclair 1995). Secondly, evaluation is the activity of screening a specific opportunity, need, or problem with regards to business objectives or general feasibility (Bernstein and Singh 2006; Majaro 1988). Thirdly, the detailing activity refers to the creation of a precise definition of the need or opportunity including an analysis of side conditions that need to be taken into account when developing possible solutions (Zairi and Sinclair 1995).

The seizing ability deals with the development and selection of solutions. For process-oriented dynamic capabilities, it is structured into three activities: (1) solution development, (2) solution evaluation and selection, and (3) solution detailing. Solution development is the activity of generating different potential solutions and, thus, different potential paths organizations could take when redesigning their corresponding operational capabilities (here: processes). As such, solution development is closely related to concept development or idea refinement. The second activity, solution evaluation, is about evaluating these different alternatives. This activity makes use of established procedures that allow informed decision making and, in the end, the selection of the most adequate solution for the problem at hand. This selected solution is detailed in the third activity (solution detailing). The first refined process descriptions need to be detailed, which includes, e.g., process modeling and the development of a comprehensive BPM project plan (Ortbach et al. 2012).

The transformation ability, which refers to the socio-technical transformation of the organization with respect to the developed and detailed solution, makes use of the three activities of (1) unfreezing, (2) changing, and (3) (re)freezing (Lewin and Cartwright 1951). Firstly, unfreezing is the activity of breaking up existing work structures. Unfreezing is an important aspect in process innovation projects. The changes and change strategies as well as the anticipated benefits have to be communicated (Kotter 2007). Secondly, changing refers to the actual implementation of process change. The central issue in the changing activity is the speed and the means with which business processes are adapted. Lastly, freezing relates to the tasks necessary to foster internalization of the new processes. It includes continuous motivation (Mento et al. 2002) and process trainings (Bashein et al. 1994).

Thus, process-oriented dynamic capabilities, e.g., Business Process Management, rely on the three abilities of sensing, seizing, and transformation (Teece 2009). These abilities each rely on three distinct activities (Ortbach et al. 2012). This relationship is depicted in Fig. 4.3.

This understanding of process-oriented dynamic capabilities is applied to the case study PHONESERV (Ortbach et al. 2012). Results suggest that the distinction

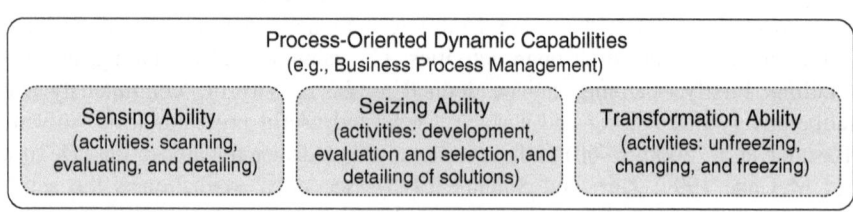

**Fig. 4.3**  Abilities used by process-oriented dynamic capabilities

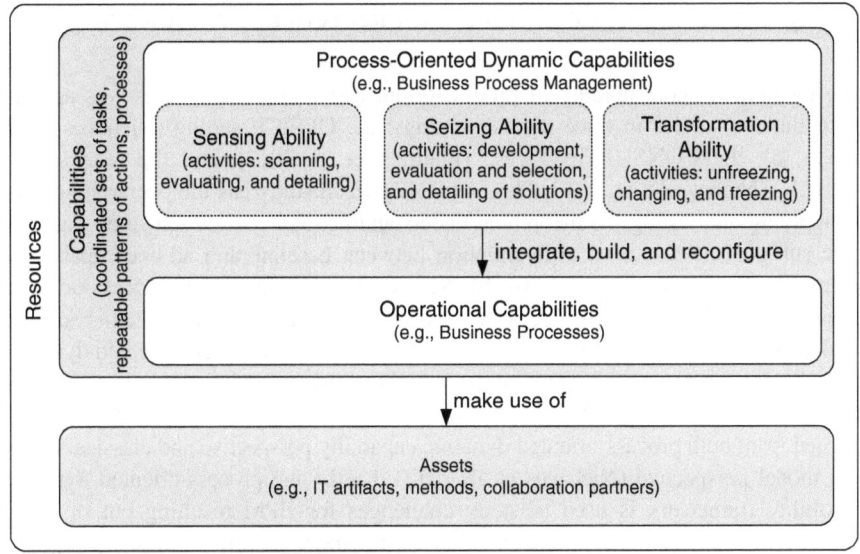

**Fig. 4.4** Process-oriented dynamic capability framework

of three abilities with three activities each is valid and useful to both structure and understand BPM and process innovation in organizations. Further need for more qualitative studies in other case settings is also expressed (Ortbach et al. 2012). This should increase the reliability of the results.

The relationships of assets, operational capabilities, dynamic capabilities, and the corresponding abilities and activities are shown in Fig. 4.4. Resources are assets or capabilities. Capabilities can be divided into dynamic and operational capabilities. (Process-oriented) dynamic capabilities rely on three abilities with three activities each.

While BPM is an example of process-oriented dynamic capabilities, it is not the only one. Next to BPM, service innovation (see Sect. 2.3) can be understood as a process-oriented dynamic capability, too. A service can be defined as "a time-perishable, intangible experience performed for a client who is acting as a coproducer to transform a state of the client" (Spohrer and Maglio 2008, p. 240). Moreover, an important characteristic of services is their process nature (Katzan 2008). Bitner et al. (2008) even argue that services can be understood as processes. As such, service provision is an operational capability. The development of new services (service innovation) borrows key concepts from the product development literature (Alam and Perry 2002; Menor et al. 2002; Shulver 2005; Stevens and Dimitriadis 2005). It is also argued that service innovation is closely related to BPM (Maleyeff 2011). Because of this and the process nature of services, service innovation can be understood as a process-oriented dynamic capability (Pöppelbuß et al. 2011b).

## 4.3  Qualitative Application of the Theoretical Framework

The theoretical understanding of process-oriented dynamic capabilities was applied in qualitative studies in three distinct settings: the OFFICE setting (Niehaves et al. 2011a, b), the CONSULTING case (Plattfaut et al. 2012), and the case setting PUBLIC (Niehaves et al. 2013; Plattfaut 2012). Each study has the overarching goal of applying and testing the theoretical understanding. Moreover, each study has specific sub-goals. As such, a differentiation between baseline and ad-hoc capabilities is introduced (Niehaves et al. 2011b). Moreover, the sourcing of process-oriented dynamic capabilities with respect to the governance structure is analyzed (Niehaves et al. 2011a). Next, service innovation is conceptualized as a process-oriented dynamic capability and the usage of operational capabilities and assets for service innovation is discussed (Plattfaut et al. 2012). Furthermore, the development of BPM capabilities is studied from both process-oriented dynamic capability perspective and classical maturity model perspective (Niehaves et al. 2013). Lastly, the process-oriented dynamic capability framework is used to study challenges for BPM resulting out of aging workforces and gaps in the corresponding employment histories (Plattfaut 2012). In this section, the main results of these five qualitative applications are presented briefly.

The differentiation of sensing, seizing, and transformation abilities that are used by process-oriented dynamic capabilities is extended with a second dimension: The degree of institutionalization of process-oriented dynamic capabilities (Niehaves et al. 2011b). Based on the original dynamic capability theory, baseline dynamic capabilities can be differentiated from ad-hoc capabilities (Winter 2003). On the one hand, baseline dynamic capabilities refer to learned and stable patterns which the organization possesses (Zollo and Winter 2002) and involve long-term commitment to specialized resources (Winter 2003). Thus, they are structured, persistent, and exist independent of a specific change event (Barreto 2009). On the other hand, ad-hoc capabilities emerge in a particular situation or change event. They are not repetitious and can be compared to "firefighting" (Helfat and Peteraf 2003; Winter 2003). This understanding is applied to two distinct process change events at OFFICE, the introduction of a new ERP system and a new customer relationship management (CRM) system. The introduction of both new systems should have led to corresponding process innovations. However, in the CRM case, new processes were only modeled in a textual form using baseline capabilities. This led to failures in seizing which prevented organizational change. In contrast, in the ERP system introduction, the baseline capabilities were extended with ad-hoc capabilities. Exemplarily, the new processes were modeled using graphical notations with the help of ad-hoc capabilities. Among other differences in capability usage, this led to a success of the ERP introduction. Thus, it could be demonstrated that the understanding of BPM as a process-oriented dynamic capability holds and is valuable in explaining the change of business processes. Often, the baseline capabilities of OFFICE were not enough to ensure change success and, thus, the organization created ad-hoc capabilities or used ad-hoc capabilities to extend baseline capabilities to succeed (Niehaves et al. 2011b).

The perception that OFFICE does not have the baseline capabilities to conduct process change is underlined by the next study (Niehaves et al. 2011a). Here, the distinction between ad-hoc process change and baseline process-oriented dynamic capabilities is mirrored with a governance dimension. All capabilities can be sourced using the governance structures market, cooperation, and hierarchy (Thorelli 1986; Williamson 1975). Results suggest that OFFICE has to rely on ad-hoc process change (Niehaves et al. 2011b). Necessary resources are sourced using all three governance types: Process change projects are carried out by the affected departments (hierarchical sourcing), they are sometimes supported through the inclusion of customers (cooperative sourcing), and the projects are often carried out with the help of external consultants to compensate a lack of know-how and manpower (market sourcing). As such, the results suggest that process innovation can be understood as a process-oriented dynamic capability according to the presented framework. Moreover, the three sourcing strategies are all used at OFFICE, although OFFICE relies mostly on ad-hoc capabilities and less on institutionalized dynamic capabilities. One possible explanation is the low dynamic market environment OFFICE is facing. Following the definition of process-oriented dynamic capabilities as an organization's abilities to change the organization's business processes in order to achieve a fit with the market environment, process-oriented dynamic capabilities are of greater use when the market environment is highly dynamic and, thus, more change is necessary (Niehaves et al. 2011a).

Based on this argument, an organization situated in a highly dynamic market environment was chosen in order to test the understanding of service innovation as a process-oriented dynamic capability: IT-CONSULT (Plattfaut et al. 2012). In the case study it could be shown that IT-CONSULT relies on abilities of sensing, seizing, and transformation. However, these abilities appear to be less institutionalized. Still, IT-CONSULT is well able to involve these abilities and the corresponding assets. This inclusion of non-institutionalized ad-hoc capabilities appears to be systemic. Again, one potential explanation is the market environment. Eisenhardt and Martin (2000) argue that dynamic capabilities differ between low-dynamic market environments and high-velocity market environments. According to their research, "dynamic capabilities in high-velocity markets are simple" (p. 1111) and make use of tacit knowledge (Eisenhardt and Martin 2000). All in all, the process-oriented dynamic capability framework is applicable to service innovation (Plattfaut et al. 2012). However, the paper calls for future, especially quantitative, research. This is addressed in Sect. 4.4.

The conceptualization of BPM as a process-oriented dynamic capability is used to study the status-quo of BPM capabilities in local governments and to assess whether BPM maturity models offer good guidance for capability development (Niehaves et al. 2013). BPM maturity models are both widely used in practice and of growing interest in research. They describe typical patterns of capability development (here: BPM development) by means of a linear sequence of stages that forms a natural path from an initial to a target maturity stage (Pöppelbuß 2012; Pöppelbuß et al. 2011a). With regards to the two research objectives, BPM was studied in terms of the six capability areas strategic alignment, governance, methods, IT, people, and culture (Rosemann and vom Brocke 2010; Rosemann and De Bruin 2005; Rosemann et al. 2006). In order to assess the status-quo, a part of the survey data set Local Administrations was analyzed descriptively (only German administrations). Results suggest that German local governments are well positioned with regards to IT and badly positioned with regards to methods. Agreement rates to questions regarding the other capability areas are on intermediate levels (Niehaves et al. 2013). Based on these results, a typical German local government was selected for qualitative analysis: PUBLIC. The qualitative analysis was needed to address the second research objective. As the BPM capabilities are on a rather low level, classical maturity models would give the advice of increasing BPM capabilities towards an ultimate level (Rosemann et al. 2006; Zwicker et al. 2010). This view on capability development can be understood as following convergence theory (Meyer et al. 1975). However, this understanding is not in line with dynamic capability theory. Dynamic capability theory calls for a development of the BPM capabilities based on the organizational positions, the paths taken in the past, and, most importantly, the dynamics of the market environment. Thus, PUBLIC should develop their BPM capabilities only to a certain extent. It could be shown that the understanding of BPM as a process-oriented dynamic capability is applicable in the public sector and useful for giving advice on capability development (Niehaves et al. 2013). This advice appears to be in contrast to classical maturity models.

The understanding of BPM as a process-oriented dynamic capability was used to explain the challenges for organizations resulting out of both societal aging (and, thus, aging workforces) and increasing gaps in the employment histories (Plattfaut 2012). Based on results gathered in PUBLIC, it could be shown that the organization has to manage the employees with respect to fluid and crystallized intelligence (Cattell 1971). Fluid intelligence refers to the capacity to think logically and to solve problems in new situations. It is independent of acquired knowledge. In contrast, crystallized intelligence is the capacity to use existing knowledge, skills, and experience (Bruch and Kunze 2007; Cattell 1971). Typically, fluid intelligence peaks in young years and decreases over time while crystallized intelligence increases with age. Both types of intelligence are needed in BPM. Firstly, in sensing, both types of intelligence are helpful. Secondly, in seizing, the organization needs larger amounts of fluid intelligence for the creative creation of new solutions. Lastly, in transformation both types are needed, too. As fluid intelligence declines over time, aging workforces pose a threat to process-oriented dynamic capabilities. Thus, organizations should manage their workforce accordingly (Plattfaut 2012).

The results of the qualitative applications of the developed theoretical process-oriented dynamic capability framework are shown in Table 4.1. While all articles had their special focus, they also made use of the theoretical framework. In all of the articles, the framework deemed to be helpful to structure. Moreover, the framework was extended with regards to the differentiation between ad-hoc change and institutionalized capabilities (Niehaves et al. 2011a, b; Plattfaut et al. 2012), it was mirrored with different governance structures (Niehaves et al. 2011a), it could serve to give a certain amount of advice with regards to capability development

**Table 4.1**   Results of the qualitative applications

|  | Case | General application | Special focus |
|---|---|---|---|
| Niehaves et al. (2011b) | OFFICE | Understanding of BPM as a process-oriented dynamic capability using sensing, seizing, and transformation abilities was used and considered valuable | Differentiation between ad-hoc change and institutionalized capabilities for change |
| Niehaves et al. (2011a) | OFFICE | Understanding of BPM as a process-oriented dynamic capability was used and is valuable | Differentiation with regards to governance structures (market, cooperation, and hierarchy) |
| Plattfaut et al. (2012) | IT-CONSULT | Understanding of service innovation as a process-oriented dynamic capability using sensing, seizing, and transformation abilities and assets was used and considered valuable | Differentiation between ad-hoc change and institutionalized capabilities for change |
| Niehaves et al. (2013) | PUBLIC | Understanding of BPM as a process-oriented dynamic capability holds and is valuable | Implications of the process-oriented dynamic capability framework for development models for BPM |
| Plattfaut (2012) | PUBLIC | Understanding of BPM as a process-oriented dynamic capability relying on the three abilities of sensing seizing, and transformation was used and considered valuable | Aging workforces and process-oriented dynamic capabilities |

(Niehaves et al. 2013), and it helped to understand the impact of aging workforces on process-oriented dynamic capabilities (Plattfaut 2012). It could also be shown that further quantitative studies are needed in order to better understand process-oriented dynamic capabilities and their governance structures.

## 4.4   Quantitative Application of the Theoretical Framework

The results of the qualitative research presented in Sect. 4.3 highlighted the need for two distinct quantitative studies. Firstly, the differentiation with regards to alternative governance structures (Niehaves et al. 2011a) and the implications of the process-oriented dynamic capability framework for BPM capability develop-ment (Niehaves et al. 2013) call for further research. Here, the factors influenc-ing the organizational choice of governance structures should be studied. Thus, a corresponding analysis of the data set Local Administrations was conducted (Niehaves et al. 2012). Secondly, quantitative research on service innovation con-ceptualized as a process-oriented dynamic capability is needed (Plattfaut et al. 2012) A theoretical model for this research is developed and analyzed with the help of the data set Service Firms (Plattfaut et al. 2013a, b). Both studies are shortly presented in the following.

The research objective of the first study is to analyze which contextual vari-ables influence the structure of BPM networks, drawing on data from the public sector (Niehaves et al. 2012). Based on arguments stated above, the influence of BPM maturity, organizational size, and financial stress on the three mechanisms of governance in BPM (hierarchy, cooperation, and market) are studied. Moreover, it is analyzed whether there are differences with regards to the country the local administrations are based in (Japan or Germany). The first influencing factor, BPM maturity covers the question, how good an organization is with regards to the six different capability areas of strategic alignment, governance, methods, IT, people, and culture (Rosemann et al. 2006). Typically, maturing organizations involve more actors from that organization (hierarchy). In addition, very mature organi-zations are said to manage their processes cooperatively (Fisher 2004; Rosemann et al. 2006). Furthermore, it can be assumed that organizations with low maturity are tempted to "buy" help for process management (market). The second independ-ent variable, organizational size refers to the amount of employees in an organi-zation. Exemplarily, it is safe to assume that smaller organizations might have problems in mobilizing enough internal resources (hierarchy). The third influenc-ing factor, financial stress refers to a self-assessment whether the financial pressure for the organization is high. As BPM projects are costly, organizations with finan-cial stress might be restricted with regards to market governance. The three govern-ance types are measured using the perceived importance of sets of corresponding actors. Examples are mayors, department heads, or employees for hierarchy, citi-zens, local government organizations, or other local governments for cooperation, and consultants or software companies for market governance (Niehaves et al. 2012). The research model and the main results are depicted in Fig. 4.5.

The descriptive results suggest that public sector organizations rely heavily on internal actors. Around two-thirds of all organizations see hierarchical actors as important (60 % in Germany, 65 % in Japan). Other governance structures (coop-eration, market) are rarely considered as being central (Niehaves et al. 2012).

PLS-SEM was used to analyze the causal relations of the research model (Ringle et al. 2012). With regards to the outer (measurement) model, valid-ity could be confirmed (Niehaves et al. 2012). With regards to the relationships between independent and dependent variables, several interesting observations could be made. Firstly, in both Germany and Japan organizations that are more mature with regards to their BPM capabilities tend to collaborate with BPM actors using all governance types. However, the influence on market governance is less

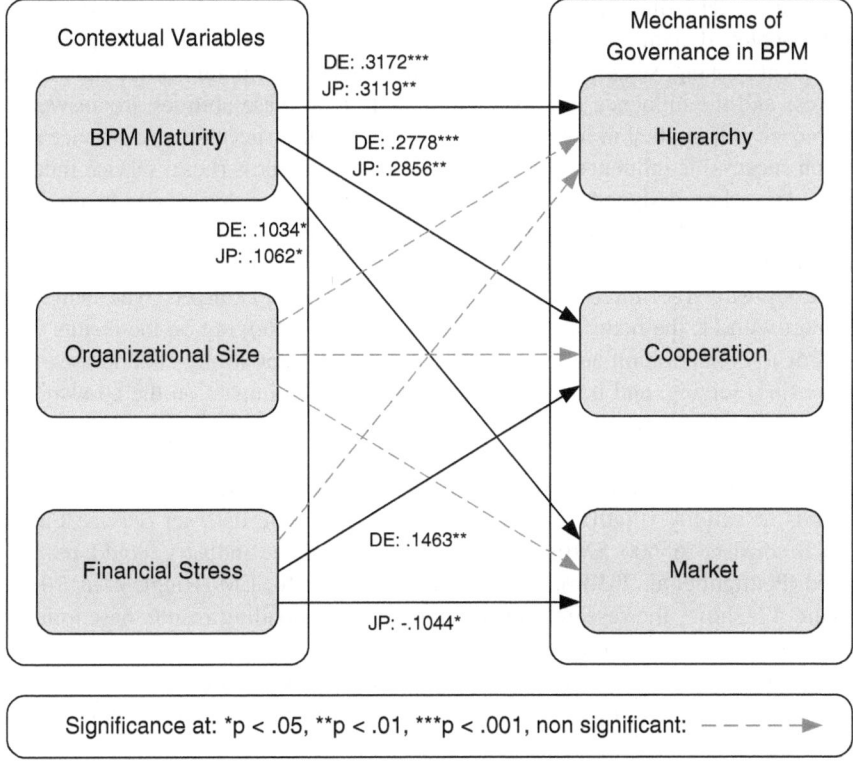

**Fig. 4.5** Influence of contextual variables on BPM governance (Niehaves et al. 2012)

significant and considerably lower. Still, this finding is conflicting with the literature which suggests that increasing maturity leads to a decrease of market sourcing
(Rosemann et al. 2006). Secondly, the impact of organizational size on governance forms is insignificant. Apparently, the choice of governance and the size are
not related to one another. Thirdly, in Germany, greater financial stress leads to a
higher employment of the governance type cooperation. It is possible that organizations in similar settings collaborate with each other when financial stress exists.
In contrast, in Japan a negative influence of financial stress on market-type governance is observable. Apparently, Japanese organizations that face financial stress are
less likely to employ market-type governance such as BPM consultants (Niehaves
et al. 2012).

As such, it could be shown that a clear relationship between BPM maturity
and collaboration with other actors inside and outside the organization exists
(Niehaves et al. 2012). Moreover, the influence of the other contextual factors, i.e.,
financial stress and organizational size, is rather low (Niehaves et al. 2012).

In the second quantitative study, a research model based on results presented
above is tested using the data set Service Firms (Plattfaut et al. 2013a, b). The

research model builds upon the conceptualization of service innovation as a process-oriented dynamic capability. With the model, research questions regarding the extent sensing, seizing, and transformation abilities explain service innovation success and the influence of collaboration and IT on these abilities are answered. Moreover, it is studied in how far operational capability success (here: service provision success) is influenced by dynamic capability success (here: service innovation). According to dynamic capability theory, this relationship should be positive. As process-oriented dynamic capabilities rely on sensing, seizing, and transformation abilities, it is hypothesized that the three abilities influence dynamic capability success positively. Moreover, the three abilities rely on IT assets. The better the support with IT, the better the organizational abilities. Relying on the results with regards to collaboration and governance, it is argued that strong collaborative ties in sensing, seizing, and transformation have a positive impact on the corresponding abilities. Furthermore, the collaborative ties are hypothesized to be stronger when corresponding IT is used to support the collaboration. This research model was tested at first with the initial data set (n = 100). As there were no issues with regards to validity (Plattfaut et al. 2013a), the complete data set Service Firms, which consists of 600 SMEs from the German service industry, could be analyzed (Plattfaut et al. 2013b). This was done using PLS-SEM (Ringle et al. 2012). Figure 4.6 shows the research model and the corresponding results based on the published article by Plattfaut et al. (2013a).

Before the structural research model (inner model) could be analyzed, the validity of the outer model had to be assessed. Here, no validity issues were

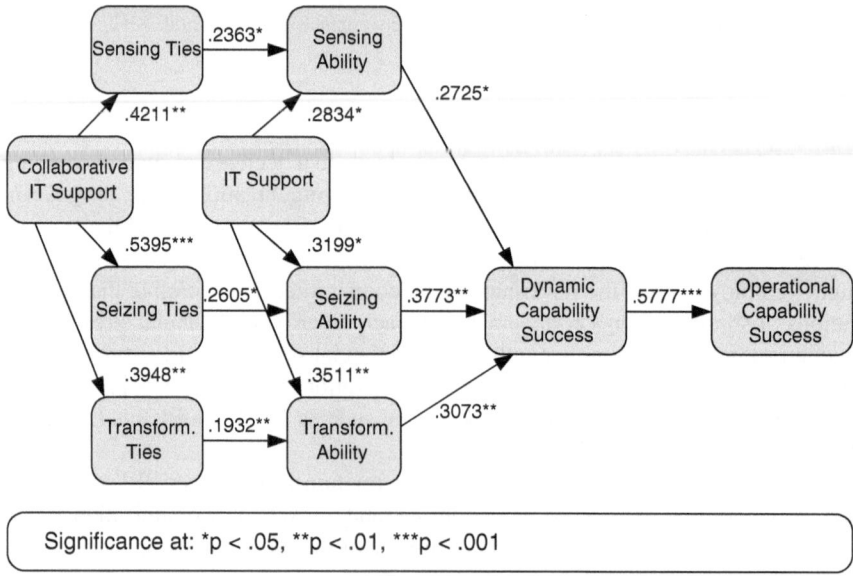

Significance at: *p < .05, **p < .01, ***p < .001

**Fig. 4.6** Collaboration, IT support, and process-oriented dynamic capabilities (Plattfaut et al. 2013a)

**Table 4.2** Coefficients of Determination (Excerpt from Plattfaut et al. 2013a)

| Dependent variable | $R^2$ |
| --- | --- |
| Operational capability success | 0.3338 |
| Dynamic capability success | 0.6470 |
| Sensing ability | 0.1893 |
| Seizing ability | 0.2377 |
| Transformation ability | 0.1862 |
| Sensing ties | 0.1773 |
| Seizing ties | 0.2910 |
| Transformation ties | 0.1559 |

observed and, thus, the constructs are valid and work as intended. The results of the inner model analysis suggest that all hypothesized relationships of the structural model are significant (Plattfaut et al. 2013a). With regards to the amount of explained variance, the coefficients of determination ($R^2$) are on a low to medium level (Table 4.2).

The analysis of the research model allows for several conclusions with regards to the developed theoretical framework (Plattfaut et al. 2013a). Firstly, in the service industry, it could be found that process-oriented dynamic capabilities (service innovation) have a substantial positive impact on operational capabilities (service provision) as about 33 % of the variance of operational capability is explained by dynamic capability success. Secondly, process-oriented dynamic capabilities rely on sensing, seizing, and transformation abilities. About 65 % of the variance in service innovation success is explained by these three antecedents. All of these relationships were positive and highly significant. Thirdly, IT support levers the three abilities. As such, it can be considered important for service innovation. Fourthly, collaboration appears to be important for sensing, seizing, and transformation, too. Stronger collaborative ties in sensing, seizing, or transformation have in fact a positive and significant influence on the corresponding abilities. However, the influence in transformation is lower. Apparently, collaboration helps organizations in building the abilities for sensing, seizing, and, to a smaller extent, in transformation. Fifthly, collaborative IT support helps in strengthening the collaborative ties. All of these path coefficients are positive and significant (Plattfaut et al. 2013a).

These results indicate that the developed theoretical framework holds a quantitative application in the service industry. It could be observed that the three abilities of sensing, seizing, and transformation are in fact used by process-oriented dynamic capabilities. Moreover, the strongest relationship is between the seizing ability and the dynamic capability success. This highlights the importance of proper service design. Moreover, process-oriented dynamic capabilities are supported by strong collaborative ties and IT usage (Plattfaut et al. 2013a, b).

The results of the applications of the theoretical framework in the service industry call for design-oriented research: Further methodological and IT support in the area of seizing appears to be helpful. A method for the first development of solutions that integrates with the other activities and abilities seems to be appropriate (Plattfaut et al. 2013b). This is in line with the literature: "Description methods and model[l]ing tools developed specifically for service engineering that are capable of supporting the complete process from end to end—from the original brainstorming and idea appraisal [sensing] through the elaboration of a concept [seizing] to the actual service implementation [transformation]—are essentially lacking" (Bullinger et al. 2003, p. 285f). The design of such a method is described in Sect. 4.5.

## 4.5  Design-Oriented Method Development

Applications of the theoretical framework in the service industry showed that methodological and technological support, especially for seizing, is valuable for successful service innovation (Plattfaut et al. 2013a, b). This support should be used in collaborative settings as collaboration was identified as one important antecedent of dynamic capability success, too. In order to address this topic, design-oriented research was conducted to develop a method (Becker et al. 2013; Voigt et al. 2013a) and a corresponding IT artifact (Becker et al. 2013; Voigt et al. 2013b). This section presents results from the mentioned prior studies and an additional overview of the functionality of the current software prototype.

The term business model refers to a conceptual model of a business idea (Voigt et al. 2013a). With the business model framework, new (service) ideas can be captured and conceptualized into a business model. According to the theoretical conceptualization of service innovation in the process-oriented dynamic capability framework, the creation of new services involves several abilities and activities. Typically, methods that support these abilities and activities differ. Exemplarily, sensing involves brainstorming tools, seizing involves process modeling techniques, and transformation makes use of project management methods. Information gathered in earlier steps of service innovation should be reused in later ones to assure project success (Bullinger et al. 2003). Moreover, as identified in the qualitative and quantitative research above, service innovation typically involves different stakeholders. A process perspective on new services helps to integrate their distinct perspective on the new service and allows for information reuse from earlier and in later stages. Thus, a process perspective should be included in a business model framework. This is especially important when the new business to be modeled is a service, as services can be understood as processes, too (Katzan 2008). As contemporary business model frameworks mainly include key activities without a relationship between them, the development (and first evaluation) of a process-oriented framework for the creation of business models in the service industry can be considered a valid research objective (Voigt et al. 2013a).

This research objective was achieved by several build and evaluate phases (March and Smith 1995). Firstly, existing business model frameworks were analyzed and integrated. Secondly, a preliminary integrated process-oriented business model framework for the service industry was developed. Thirdly, the framework was tested with the help of students and, fourthly, modified based on their feedback. Fifthly, the model was evaluated by several practitioners which led to another build iteration (Voigt et al. 2013a). Moreover, the resulting business model framework is presented and evaluated through a retrospective application to a real-world service innovation (Voigt et al. 2013a). This framework is called ProcBiz.

The developed method has to be supported by a collaborative IT artifact in order to be used by organizations in their service innovation processes independent of time and location of the corresponding employees. Moreover, the quantitative study of the data set Service Firms could show that there is a positive relationship between collaborative IT usage and service innovation success. The method is presented in a more practitioner-oriented way by Becker et al. (2013) and Malsbender et al. (2013). More importantly, the developed IT artifact is introduced (Becker et al. 2013). The latest state of the process-oriented business model framework for the service industry is presented in the following. It is a slightly updated version of earlier work (Becker et al. 2013; Voigt et al. 2013a).

ProcBiz is a process-oriented business modeling framework that is used to conceptualize new service ideas in order to be able to compare and evaluate those ideas before implementing them. As such, it supports the seizing ability and is used in solution development, evaluation, and selection activities. The framework consists of seven components (Fig. 4.7)[1]: the service provision process, value propositions, resources, financials, central functions, central resources, and fixed financials. These seven components were selected for two main reasons: Firstly, as argued above, ProcBiz is process-oriented. Hence, the process steps and central functions are needed. One of the main questions in process-orientation is to identify which solutions actually create value (Harmon 2007). Thus, a value component is needed in process-oriented business modeling. Feedback from modelers in the build and evaluate cycles led to a division of the value component into customer and business values. Secondly, in order to evaluate and select a specific business model, decision makers rely on a profitability assessment (Amit and Zott 2001; Lee 2001). Thus, financials and fixed financials have to be included. Moreover, it is necessary to explicate the resources required in the process in order to lever reliability of the financial estimates. Hence, a resource component is needed.

The focal point of the framework is formed by the process component and the central functions component. Elements in all other components are organized in rows referring to elements from the process component and the central functions component (e.g., Expense 2, Resource 2, and Value 1 belong to Activity 2 in Fig. 4.7). This enhances readability and understandability of the business model.

In the process component, the service provision process is described as an interaction between the service provider and the service customer facilitated by channels. Customer and business activities are modeled separately (e.g., Activity 1 and Activity 2 in Fig. 4.7). Channels refer to both technical and personal communication, e.g., via telephone, e-mail, or electronic data interchange. The process component allows for straightforward process modeling without branching or looping.

---

[1] A conceptual meta-model of ProcBiz can be found in the appendix.

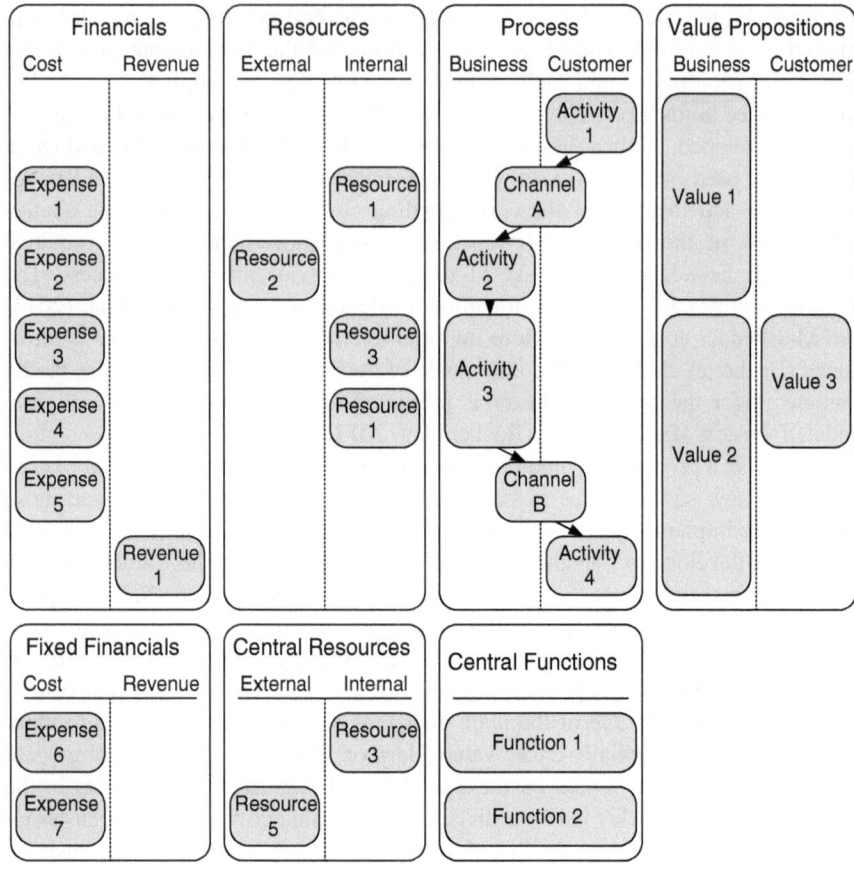

**Fig. 4.7** The process-oriented business modeling framework ProcBiz

Modelers should be able to refine the resulting "coarse-grained" process in later stages of the service innovation process, e.g., in the solution detailing activity.

The value proposition component allows for the definition of both customer values (Timmers 1998) and business values (Betz 2002). The values are related to process activities and channels. This allows for an identification of process steps that do not deliver any value. A value may be related to more than one activity (e.g., Value 1 in Fig. 4.7). Vice versa, one activity may be related to more than one value (e.g., Activity 3 in Fig. 4.7).

In the resource component, internal and external resources required for the performance of the process activities and implementing the channels are defined. Internal resources refer to those owned by the organization. External resources are goods and services provided by external partners. Resources can be used by more than one activity (e.g., Resource 1 in Fig. 4.7). An activity can make use of multiple resources (e.g., Activity 3 in Fig. 4.7).

The financials component contains all costs and revenues of one single service provision. Here, the modeler might have to rely on averaged values. The financials component should provide basic but internally consistent information on the overall profits and losses of the new service. Financials can be defined for resources (e.g., Expense 1 in Fig. 4.7) or independent of resources (e.g., Expense 5 in Fig. 4.7). However, costs and revenues always refer to a specific process activity or channel.

The central functions component contains all business functions that are independent of one single service provision but needed for performing them. They correspond to support processes such as IT services or human resource management (Harmon 2007).

Central resources are resources that are used by central functions. Again, central resources can be divided in internal and external resources. A central function can have multiple resources. Moreover, a resource can be used by multiple central functions or by central functions and process steps (e.g., Resource 3 in Fig. 4.7).

The fixed financials component is comparable to the financial component. Costs and revenues are modeled relating to central functions or resources (e.g., Expense 6 in Fig. 4.7.) Here, the financials are considered fixed with respect to a certain time horizon, e.g., per year. This allows for further financial analyses.

Additionally, there are other figures the business modeler has to estimate. These include the one time investments needed to start the new service and the number of process iterations in a certain period of time.

An initial financial evaluation of the new service can be calculated using the estimated figures. These include, e.g., the contribution margin of a single service provision, the total contribution margin, the profit/loss per period, and the time of break-even.

The information gathered with the help of the process-oriented business modeling framework ProcBiz can be reused in later service innovation phases. Exemplarily, the "coarse-grained" process can be refined in process models or service blueprints prior to organizational service implementation. Moreover, the financial information could be used for further calculations in terms of business casing.

Furthermore, an ex-post application of ProcBiz to a real-life business idea in the case organization OFFICE was conducted (Voigt et al. 2013a). In this example, the new service idea was implemented in the organization without proper business modeling. The financial results of the service were unsatisfying for decision makers and the service was regarded as a failure. The application of ProcBiz would have helped to estimate the financial contribution and, thus, to lower expectations. Moreover, the value contributions for customer and business would have been explicated.

Next, a software prototype of ProcBiz is introduced (Becker et al. 2013). The current prototype is named OctoProz and was created between March 2012 and February 2013 by a team of students and research assistants. The implementation team consisted of 21 members. OctoProz is an implementation of the ProcBiz modeling method.[2] It was built using the Ruby on Rails framework and other

---

[2] A conceptual meta-model of the ProcBiz modeling method is presented in the appendix. The data model of OctoProz builds upon this meta-model.

state-of-the-art technology. Thus, OctoProz is a browser-based application that employs interactive controls and drag-and-drop functionality. Users can create new business models including all seven components.

The modeling environment of OctoProz is depicted in Fig. 4.8. In the center of the screen, the modeler can create the business model using the ProcBiz methodology described above. The color of all model elements can be changed by the user which allows highlighting of important aspects. Activities and channels have a title, a description, and a duration. Finance elements can be time-dependent (marked with a clock) or independent of time. Fixed financial elements work accordingly. They can occur per month, quarter, or year.

The top buttons allow the user to open a wizard (help) which guides the creation of a new business model. The undo/redo-buttons are used to correct mistakes in the modeling process. The finance button has two different options. Firstly, the user can color all rows of the business model according to their sum of costs and revenues. Activities with high costs are shown in dark red, those with high revenues in bright green. Thus, the modeler can easily assess financially critical activities in the business model. Secondly, the user can open a financial analysis module (Fig. 4.9) which will be described later. The syntax check button opens the syntax check view on the right. Potential errors are indicated, e.g., when resources are not

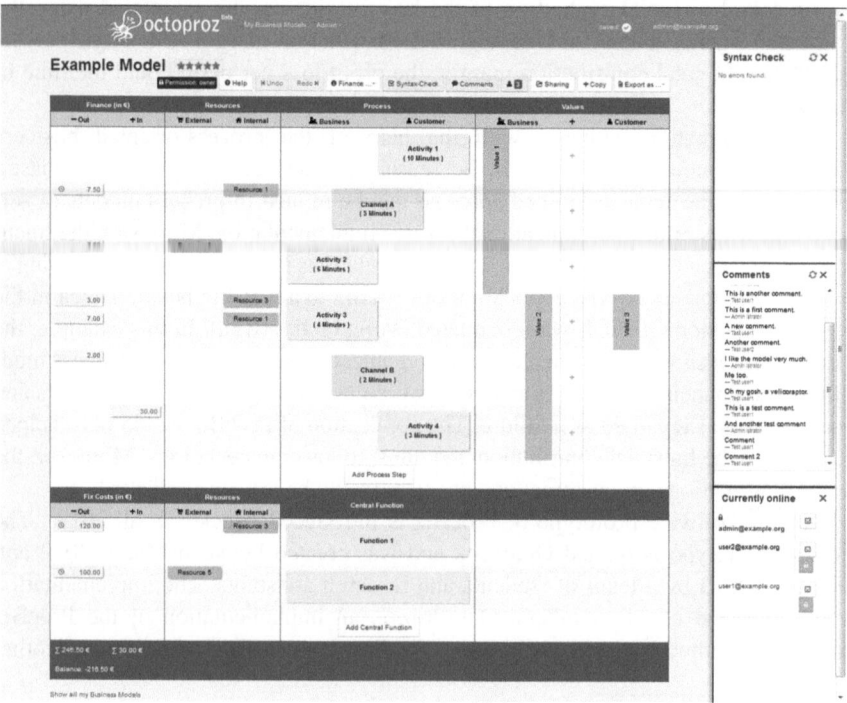

**Fig. 4.8** OctoProz: modeling environment

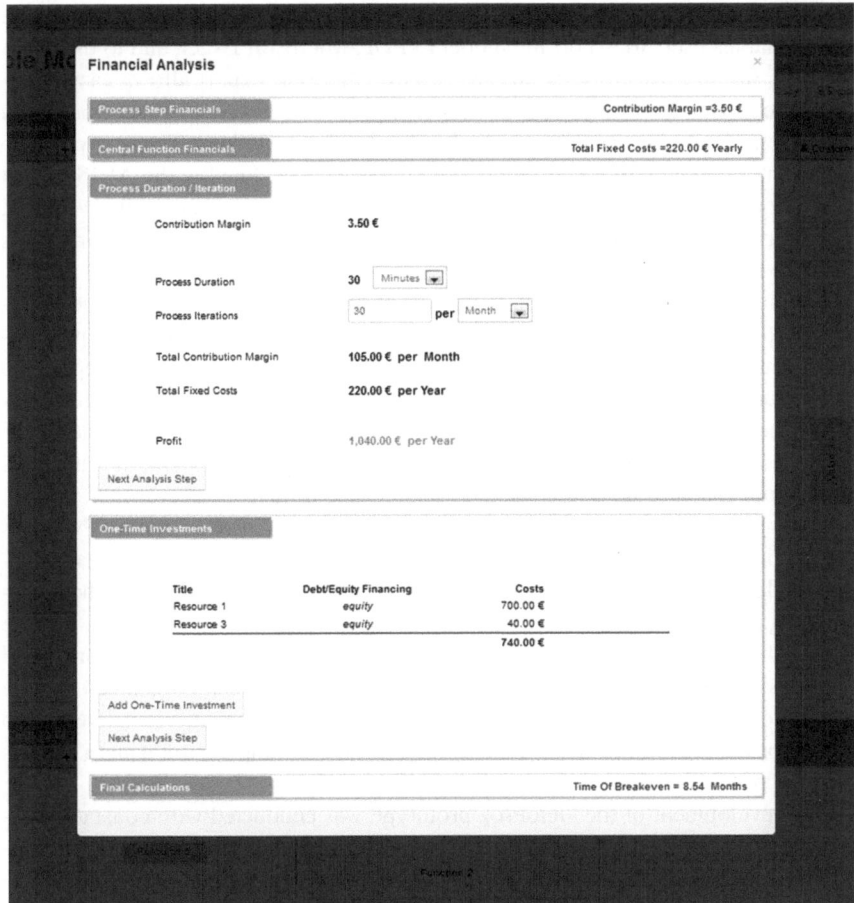

**Fig. 4.9** OctoProz: financial analysis

associated with costs. However, the user can always opt to ignore these alerts in order to maximize modeling freedom. The comments button opens the comments view on the right. Here, each model user can comment on the model in plain text, independent of their corresponding rights. Next, the currently online button informs all users about other users currently watching the model. The model is locked by the first user with write or owner rights when opening the model. Only this user can edit the model. The changes are pushed to the watching users in real time. The locking user can also transfer the lock to other users with the appropriate rights when clicking on the yellow transfer lock button. The sharing button allows users to share the model with other users. Therefore, the owner of the business model has to enter a valid e-mail address and has to select between read, write, and owner rights. An invitation is sent to the collaborator. Users with read rights cannot edit the model. Users with write rights are allowed to edit the model.

The copy button allows users to create personal copies of the model. The export button enables users to export the model to PDF, Microsoft Excel, and to the ARIS Business Architect from Software AG. Firstly, the PDF export allows easy printing of the model. Secondly, with the Excel export the user can use the information gathered in the business model for further financial calculations. The user can also edit business models in Excel and re-import them later. Finally, the ARIS export allows for detailed process modeling. In the upper left corner of the window, each user can also rate the model on a one to five star scale. The average rating is shown to all users.

The financial analysis module (Fig. 4.9) allows a first evaluation of the financials of the business model. In five sub-steps, the user can analyze the process-dependent financials (what are the costs of resources and process steps), the central function financials (what are the fixed costs of central resources and functions), the process duration and iteration (how often is the service provided), the one-time investments (what are the set-up costs of the new service), and the final calculations (what is the return on investment or the time of breakeven).

The model management screen (Fig. 4.10) can be reached via the my business models link in the top bar or directly after logging into OctoProz. Here, all business models the user can see are listed with their name, description, tag, the corresponding permission of the user, information on the date of the last update, and the rating. The user can sort business models with regards to all these categories and search using the search field in the last row. Business models are organized using a tag to allow the comparison of related models. The model management screen also allows for the creation of new business models and the import of business models from Microsoft Excel.

The development of the OctoProz prototype was conducted with constant feedback from practitioners from multiple organizations. Their experience and suggestions were used to create the user interface and specific functionalities. The prototype is still in a beta version.

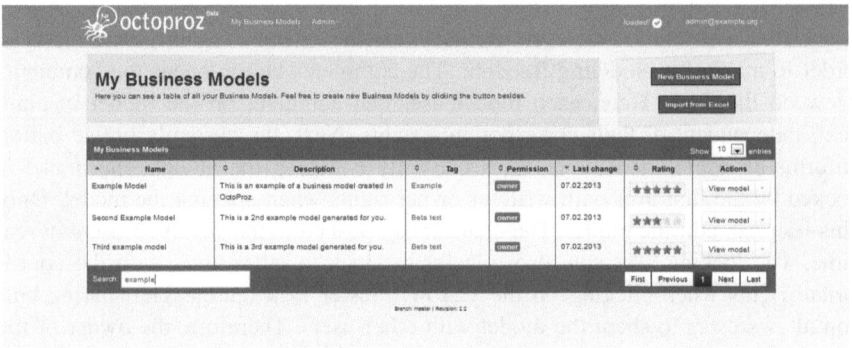

**Fig. 4.10** OctoProz: model management

## 4.6 Experimental Evaluation of the Developed Method

In order to evaluate the method to create process-oriented business models for service organizations (ProcBiz) in a rigor way, a laboratory experiment was conducted (Voigt et al. 2013c).

For the experiment, the creative potential of 81 participants was measured (Gough and Heilbrun 1965) and used to organize them in 27 groups of roughly the same average creative potential. Thirteen of these groups were trained with the ProcBiz framework. The other 14 groups received an "alternative treatment" without process-orientation and were trained in the BMC, a widely-used quasi-standard (Osterwalder and Pigneur 2010). Each group was given the same task of modeling a given business idea on a brown paper canvas containing the blank business model framework. The idea was described as a case of an office supply company that wanted to investigate the introduction of an IT-based service. Potential customers of this service were organizers of conferences which should receive ready-to-use conference badges for each conference participant. The design and ordering of the badges should be facilitated by a web-shop. Each group had one hour to create a business model based on the business idea. Afterwards, each group member completed a questionnaire including quantitative feedback with regards to the participant's satisfaction. The developed business models were digitalized and sent to an industry expert with high experience in business model assessment. This expert was a start-up consultant and innovation manager affiliated with a regional business incubator. The expert answered questionnaires for each of the models with regards to the quality of the business model content and the quality of the business model presentation (Voigt et al. 2013c).

According to the arguments presented above, it was hypothesized that models created with ProcBiz are more feasible, relevant, consistent, and comprehensible for the expert, while, at the same time, the satisfaction of the participants was higher with regards to the process and the outcome. Moreover, it was argued that the participants enjoyed the business modeling process more when ProcBiz was used. In contrast, as the business modeling process appears to be more structured when using ProcBiz it was hypothesized that the resulting business models would not be considered as novel as the ones created using BMC (Voigt et al. 2013c).

The quantitative data derived from the questionnaires answered by the participants and the expert were analyzed using independent samples t-tests. The results are presented in Table 4.3.

Novelty refers to the degree to which a business model is original and radically new. As process-orientation imposes certain restrictions on the model designer, it was argued that models created using ProcBiz are less novel. However, the results suggest that the choice between BMC and ProcBiz does not influence the novelty of the resulting models significantly. Here, the effect might be too small to be uncovered by the given sample size. Feasibility of the model is provided if the business model can be implemented easily without violating any known constraints. Process-oriented business models should be more feasible, as

**Table 4.3**  Extract of the results of the experimental evaluation

| Independent variable | Data source | Hypothesis | Result |
|---|---|---|---|
| Novelty | Expert | Lower for ProcBiz | No significant difference |
| Feasibility | Expert | Higher for ProcBiz | No significant difference |
| Relevance | Expert | Higher for ProcBiz | Higher for ProcBiz |
| Consistency | Expert | Higher for ProcBiz | Higher for ProcBiz |
| Comprehension | Expert | Higher for ProcBiz | Higher for ProcBiz |
| Outcome satisfaction | Designer | Higher for ProcBiz | No significant difference |
| Group process satisfaction | Designer | Higher for ProcBiz | No significant difference |
| Group process enjoyment | Designer | Higher for ProcBiz | Higher for ProcBiz |

the information is easier to be reused (e.g., refining coarse grained processes or further calculations of financial aspects). Although the results show higher feasibility of models created using ProcBiz, these results are not significant. Again, a reason might be the given sample size. Relevance is the degree to which the business model concept builds upon the specifics of the original idea. Here, process-orientation might help the modeler to focus. Thus, it was argued that business models created with ProcBiz are more consistent. This hypothesis is underlined by the results. Novelty, feasibility, and relevance refer to the quality of the business model content. All in all, results are mixed: Only with regards to relevance a significantly higher content quality is observable (Voigt et al. 2013c).

Consistency is the semantic fit of elements (e.g., specific activities) to the components (e.g., the process component) of the business model framework. Due to the process-orientation and row-organization it was argued that business models created with ProcBiz are more consistent than those created with BMC. This argument is supported by the data analysis. Comprehension is the understandability of the information presented in the business model. As the row-organization of ProcBiz makes the layout clearer when compared to business models created with BMC, it was argued that the corresponding models are easier to comprehend. The data analysis shows that this hypothesis cannot be falsified. As comprehension and consistency are the two main variables for the quality of the business model presentation, it can be argued that the presentation quality of business models is higher when they are created with the process-oriented business model framework ProcBiz (Voigt et al. 2013c).

In line with the arguments regarding model quality and presentation, it was hypothesized that the modelers are more satisfied with the modeling outcome when using ProcBiz. However, in the study no significant difference in outcome satisfaction could be identified. The existing difference in mean values is comparably small. Thus, the satisfaction with the outcome does not depend on the business model framework but on other external variables. Moreover, it was argued that the structure given through the process-orientation leads to a higher satisfaction of the modelers with the group process. Again, there was only a small not significant difference. Hence, the satisfaction with the modeling process does not depend on the business model framework. Finally, it was also hypothesized that modelers using

ProcBiz experience a higher enjoyment of the group process and are less bored. The study revealed strong support for this hypothesis: The mean enjoyment of the group process was significantly higher for ProcBiz-users than for those participants using BMC (Voigt et al. 2013c).

All in all, the laboratory experiment could show that ProcBiz works better than the widely accepted BMC with regards to relevance, consistency, and comprehension of the model as well as the modelers' enjoyment of the group process. Moreover, it did not perform significantly worse in any other category. Thus, the business modeling method developed based on the process-oriented dynamic capability framework, the qualitative and quantitative applications, and the direct feedback of practitioners appears to be appropriate and valuable for service innovation (Voigt et al. 2013c).

# References

Alam, I., & Perry, C. (2002). A customer-oriented new service development process. *Journal of Services Marketing, 16*(6), 515–534.

Alter, S. (2002). The work system method for understanding information systems and information system research. *Communications of the Association for Information Systems (AIS), 9*(6), 90–104.

Amit, R., & Schoemaker, P. (1993). Strategic assets and organizational rent. *Strategic Management Journal, 14*(1), 33–46.

Amit, R., & Zott, C. (2001). Value creation in e-business. *Strategic Management Journal, 22*(6–7), 493–520.

Armistead, C., & Machin, S. (1997). Implications of business process management for operations management. *International Journal of Operations and Production Management, 17*(9), 886–898.

Armistead, C., & Machin, S. (1998). Business process management: Implications for productivity in multi-stage service networks. *International Journal of Service Industry Management, 9*(4), 323–336.

Barney, J. B. (1991). Firm resources and sustained competitive advantage. *Journal of Management, 17*(1), 99–120.

Barreto, I. (2009). Dynamic capabilities: A review of past research and an agenda for the future. *Journal of Management, 36*(1), 256–280.

Basadur, M., Pringle, P., Speranzini, G., & Bacot, M. (2000). Collaborative problem solving through creativity in problem definition: Expanding the pie. *Creativity and Innovation Management, 9*(1), 54–76.

Bashein, B. J., Markus, M. L., & Riley, P. (1994). Preconditions for BPR success and how to prevent failures. *Information Systems Management, 11*(2), 7–13.

Becker, J., Malsbender, A., Ortbach, K., Plattfaut, R., Voigt, M., Höhenberger, S., et al. (2013). Business modeling—Geschäftsmodelle prozessorientiert und kollaborativ entwickeln. *Zeitschrift Führung + Organisation, 82*(2), 137–145.

Bergman, M., King, J. L., & Lyytinen, K. (2002). Large-scale requirements analysis revisited: The need for understanding the political ecology of requirements engineering. *Requirements Engineering, 7*(3), 152–171.

Bernstein, B., & Singh, P. (2006). An integrated innovation process model based on practices of Australian biotechnology firms. *Technovation, 26*(5–6), 561–572.

Betz, F. (2002). Strategic business models. *Engineering Management Journal, 14*(1), 21–27.

Bhave, M. (1994). A process model of entrepreneurial venture creation. *Journal of Business Venturing, 9*(3), 223–242.

Bitner, M. J., Ostrom, A. L., & Morgan, F. N. (2008). Service blueprinting: A practical technique for service innovation. *California Management Review, 50*(3), 66–95.

Bowman, C., & Ambrosini, V. (2003). How the resource-based and the dynamic capability views of the firm inform corporate-level strategy. *British Journal of Management, 14*(4), 289–303.

Bruch, H., & Kunze, F. (2007). Management einer aging workforce: Ansätze zu Kultur und Führung. *Zeitschrift Führung + Organisation*, 76(2), 72–77.

Bullinger, H.-J., Fähnrich, K.-P., & Meiren, T. (2003). Service engineering: Methodical development of new service products. *International Journal of Production Economics, 85*(3), 275–287.

Cattell, R. B. (1971). *Abilities: Their structure, growth, and action.* Boston: Houghton Mifflin.

Collis, D. J. (1994). Research note: How valuable are organizational capabilities? *Strategic Management Journal, 15*(1), 143–152.

Daniel, E. M., & Wilson, H. N. (2003). The role of dynamic capabilities in e-business transformation. *European Journal of Information Systems, 12*(4), 282–296.

DeToro, I., & McCabe, T. (1997). How to stay flexible and elude fads. *Quality Progress, 30*(3), 55–60.

Eisenhardt, K. M., & Martin, J. A. (2000). Dynamic capabilities: What are they? *Strategic Management Journal, 21*(10–11), 1105–1121.

Fisher, D. M. (2004). The business process maturity model: A practical approach for identifying opportunities for optimization. *Business Process Trends, 9*(4), 13.

Gough, H. G., & Heilbrun, A. B. J. (1965). *The adjective check list manual.* Palo Alto: Consulting Psychologists Press.

Harmon, P. (2007). *Business process change* (2nd ed.). Burlington: Morgan Kaufmann.

Helfat, C. E., & Peteraf, M. A. (2003). The dynamic resource-based view: Capability lifecycles. *Strategic Management Journal, 24*(10), 997–1010.

Katzan, H. (2008). Service science: Concepts, technology, management. New York: iUniverse.

Kim, G., Shin, B., Kim, K. K., & Lee, H. G. (2011). IT capabilities, process-oriented dynamic capabilities, and firm financial performance. *Journal of the Association for Information Systems (AIS), 12*(7), 487–517.

Koch, H. (2010). Developing dynamic capabilities in electronic marketplaces: A cross-case study. *The Journal of Strategic Information Systems, 19*(1), 28–38.

Kotter, J. P. (2007). Leading change: Why transformation efforts fail. *Harvard Business Review, Jan*, 92–107.

Learned, E. P., Christensen, C. R., Andrews, K. R., & Guth, W. D. (1969). *Business policy: Text and cases* (2nd ed.). Homewood: Irwin.

Lee, C.-S. (2001). An analytical framework for evaluating e-commerce business models and strategies. *Internet Research, 11*(4), 349–359.

Lewin, K., & Cartwright, D. (1951). *Field theory in social science.* New York: Harper & Brothers.

Lyytinen, K., & Newman, M. (2008). Explaining information systems change: A punctuated socio-technical change model. *European Journal of Information Systems, 17*(6), 589–613.

Lyytinen, K., Mathiassen, L., & Kuula, M. (1996). A framework for software risk management. *Journal of Information Technology, 11*(4), 275–287.

Majaro, S. (1988). *The creative gap: Managing ideas for profit.* London: Longman Trade/ Caroline House.

Maleyeff, J. (2011). Factors impacting innovation in new service offerings. *Journal of Service Science and Management, 4*(2), 111–117.

Malsbender, A., Ortbach, K., Plattfaut, R., Voigt, M., & Niehaves, B. (2013). Process-oriented business modeling—An application in the printing industry. In *International IFIP Working Conference on Enterprise Interoperability—Workshop on Interoperability to Support Business-IT Alignment*, Twente. Netherlands.

March, S. T., & Smith, G. F. (1995). Design and natural science research on information technology. *Decision Support Systems, 15*(4), 251–266.

Menor, L. J., Tatikonda, M. V., & Sampson, S. E. (2002). New service development: Areas for exploitation and exploration. *Journal of Operations Management, 20*(2), 135–157.

Mento, A., Jones, R., & Dirndorfer, W. (2002). A change management process: Grounded in both theory and practice. *Journal of Change Management, 3*(1), 45–59.

Meyer, J. W., Boli-Bennett, J., & Chase-Dunn, C. (1975). Convergence and divergence in development. *Annual Review of Sociology, 1*(1), 223–246.

Niehaves, B., & Plattfaut, R. (2011). Collaborative business process management: Status Quo and Quo Vadis. *Business Process Management Journal, 17*(3), 384–402.

Niehaves, B., Plattfaut, R., & Becker, J. (2010). Does your business process management (still) fit the market?—A dynamic capability perspective on BPM strategy development. In *Proceedings of the 16th Americas Conference on Information Systems (AMCIS)*, Lima, Peru.

Niehaves, B., Plattfaut, R., Budde, M., & Becker, J. (2011a). Business process governance: A qualitative case study at production. In *Proceedings of the 17th Americas Conference on Information Systems (AMCIS)*, Detroit, USA.

Niehaves, B., Plattfaut, R., & Sarker, S. (2011b). Understanding dynamic IS capabilities for effective process change: A theoretical framework and an empirical application. In *Proceedings of the 32nd International Conference on Information Systems (ICIS)*, Shanghai, China.

Niehaves, B., Plattfaut, R., & Becker, J. (2012). Business process governance: A comparative study of Germany and Japan. *Business Process Management Journal, 18*(2), 347–371.

Niehaves, B., Plattfaut, R., & Becker, J. (2013). Business process management capabilities in local governments: A multi-method study. *Government Information Quarterly, 30*(3), 217–225.

Ortbach, K., Plattfaut, R., Pöppelbuß, J., & Niehaves, B. (2012). A dynamic capability-based framework for business process management: Theorizing and empirical application. In *Proceedings of the 45th Hawaii International Conference on System Sciences (HICSS)*, Maui, USA.

Osterwalder, A., & Pigneur, Y. (2010). *Business model generation*. New Jersey: Wiley.

Penrose, E. P. (1959). *The theory of the growth of the firm*. Oxford: Blackwell Publishing Ltd.

Plattfaut, R. (2012). Diskontinuierliche Erwerbsbiografien und alternde Belegschaften als Herausforderung für das Management von Prozessen in der Verwaltung. *Verwaltung and Management, 18*(4), 218–222.

Plattfaut, R., Niehaves, B., & Becker, J. (2012). Capabilities for service innovation: A qualitative case study in the consulting industry. In *Proceedings of the 16th Pacific Asia Conference on Information Systems (PACIS)*, Ho Chi Minh City, Vietnam.

Plattfaut, R., Niehaves, B., Voigt, M., Malsbender, A., Ortbach, K., & Pöppelbuß, J. (2013a). IT and collaboration in service innovation: A dynamic capability perspective. In *Proceedings of the 21st European Conference for Information Systems (ECIS)*, Utrecht, Netherlands.

Plattfaut, R., Niehaves, B., Voigt, M., Malsbender, A., Ortbach, K., & Pöppelbuß, J. (2013b). *What makes service innovation successful? A dynamic capability perspective*. Unpublished manuscript.

Pöppelbuß, J. (2012). *Business process management in service networks—Capability assessment and improvement*. Dissertation. Wirtschaftswissenschaftliche Fakultät. Westfälische Wilhelms-Universität Münster.

Pöppelbuß, J., Niehaves, B., Simons, A., & Becker, J. (2011a). Maturity models in information systems research: Literature search and analysis. *Communications of the AIS, 29*(Article 27), 505–527.

Pöppelbuß, J., Plattfaut, R., Ortbach, K., Malsbender, A., Voigt, M., Niehaves, B., et al. (2011b). Service innovation capability: Proposing a new framework. In *Proceedings of the 3rd International Symposium on Services Science (ISSS) in conjunction with the Federated Conference on Computer Science and Information Systems (FedCSIS)*, Szczecin, Poland.

Pritchard, J.-P., & Armistead, C. (1999). Business process management—Lessons from European business. *Business Process Management Journal, 5*(1), 10–32.

Ringle, C. M., Sarstedt, M., & Straub, D. (2012). Editor's comments—A critical look at the use of PLS-SEM in MIS quarterly. *MIS Quarterly, 36*(1), iii–xiv.

Rosemann, M., & De Bruin, T. (2005). Towards a business process management maturity model. In *Proceedings of the 13th European Conference on Information Systems (ECIS)*, Regensburg, Germany, pp. 521–532.

Rosemann, M., & vom Brocke, J. (2010). The six core elements of business process management," In J. vom Brocke & M. Rosemann (Eds.), *Handbook on business process management
1* (pp. 107–122). Berlin/Heidelberg: Springer.

Rosemann, M., De Bruin, T., & Power, B. (2006). A model to measure business process management maturity and improve performance. In J. Jeston & J. Nelis (Eds.), *Business process
management: Practical guidelines to successful implementations* (pp. 299–315). Butterworth
Heinemann: Burlington.

Shulver, M. (2005). Operational loss and new service design. *International Journal of Service
Industry Management, 16*(5), 455–479.

Spohrer, J. C., & Maglio, P. P. (2008). The emergence of service science: Toward systematic service innovations to accelerate co-creation of value. *Production and Operations Management,
17*(3), 238–246.

Stevens, E., & Dimitriadis, S. (2005). Managing the new service development process: Towards a
systemic model. *European Journal of Marketing, 39*(1–2), 175–198.

Teece, D. J. (2009). *Dynamic capabilities and strategic management: Organizing for innovation
and growth.* Oxford: Oxford University Press.

Teece, D. J., Pisano, G., & Shuen, A. (1997). Dynamic capabilities and strategic management.
*Strategic Management Journal, 18*(7), 509–533.

Thorelli, H. B. (1986). Networks: Between markets and hierarchies. *Strategic Management
Journal, 7*(1), 37–51.

Timmers, P. (1998). Business models for electronic markets. *Electronic Markets, 8*(2), 3–8.

Trkman, P. (2010). The critical success factors of business process management. *International
Journal of Information Management, 30*(2), 125–134.

Voigt, M., Fordey, M., Malsbender, A., Ortbach, K., Plattfaut, R., & Niehaves, B. (2013a).
*Business modeling needs process-orientation—Framework development and testing.*
Unpublished manuscript.

Voigt, M., Ortbach, K., Plattfaut, R., & Niehaves, B. (2013b). Developing creative business models—The OctoProz tool. In *8th International Conference on Design Science Research in
Information Systems and Technology (DESRIST)*, Helsinki, Finland, pp. 456–462.

Voigt, M., Plattfaut, R., Ortbach, K., Malsbender, A., & Niehaves, B. (2013c). *Does business
modeling benefit from process-thinking? Insights from a group experiment.* Unpublished
manuscript.

Wade, M., & Hulland, J. (2004). Review: The resource-based view and information systems
research: Review, extension and suggestions for future research. *MIS Quarterly, 28*(1),
107–142.

Wernerfelt, B. (1984). A resource-based view of the firm. *Strategic Management Journal, 5*(2),
171–180.

Williamson, O. E. (1975). *Markets and hierarchies: Analysis and antitrust implications.* New
York: Free Press.

Winter, S. G. (2003). Understanding dynamic capabilities. *Strategic Management Journal,
24*(10), 991–995.

Zairi, M. (1997). Business process management: A boundaryless approach to modern competitiveness. *Business Process Management Journal, 3*(1), 64–80.

Zairi, M., & Sinclair, D. (1995). Business process re-engineering and process management: A
survey of current practice and future trends in integrated management. *Business Process
Re-engineering and Management Journal, 1*(1), 8–30.

Zollo, M., & Winter, S. G. (2002). Deliberate learning and the evolution of dynamic capabilities.
*Organization Science, 13*(3), 339–351.

Zwicker, J., Fettke, P., & Loos, P. (2010). Business process maturity in public administrations. In
J. vom Brocke & M. Rosemann (Eds.), *Handbook on business process management 2* (pp.
369–400). Berlin/Heidelberg: Springer.

# Chapter 5
# Discussion

## 5.1 Contributions to Theory

This SpringerBrief offers several contributions to theory in accordance with the three research questions that are presented in the following.

A theoretical framework of process-oriented dynamic capabilities was developed. This framework builds upon the dynamic capability theory. It could be shown that both BPM and service innovation can be understood as process-oriented dynamic capabilities in the sense of the framework. BPM is a set of organizational abilities to change (e.g., integrate, build, reconfigure, improve, adapt, adjust, refresh, renew, etc.) the organization's business processes in order to achieve a fit with the market environment. Service innovation can be understood similarly but with a focus on the creation of new services (and corresponding service processes). Process-oriented dynamic capabilities make use of the three abilities sensing, seizing, and transformation. In turn, these abilities rely on three distinct activities each. This understanding of process-oriented dynamic capabilities is new and forms, thus, the first contribution to theory.

Moreover, the theoretical framework was applied in qualitative and quantitative studies. These applications helped in refining the framework and showed that it is applicable and useful. The framework helps to structure, organize, and understand BPM and service innovation. Moreover, the process-oriented dynamic capability framework serves to analyze other specific issues such as capability development, capability sourcing, or the influences of aging workforces. The empirical applications of the theoretical framework resulted in two more main contributions to theory: the insufficiency of BPM maturity models and the importance of collaboration in process-oriented dynamic capabilities. Firstly, according to dynamic capability theory organizations have to adapt their operational capabilities in order to achieve a fit with the market environment. As the number of corresponding change incidents correlates with the degree of market dynamics, organizations in high velocity markets need more and better dynamic capabilities than organizations in low dynamic markets. Hence, the "optimal maturity level" of BPM as a process-oriented dynamic capability cannot be defined in a BPM maturity model but depends on the dynamics of the market environment. Thus, contemporary BPM maturity models are insufficient to guide the development of BPM abilities in organizations. This theoretical argument could be supported by results from a case study in the public sector. Secondly, process-oriented dynamic capabilities are more successful in collaborative settings. This could be supported in several case studies and, more important, in a quantitative analysis of the German service industry.

Based on the applications of the process-oriented dynamic capability framework in empirical studies, a method for the creation of process-oriented business models (ProcBiz) was designed and tested. In a laboratory experiment it could be shown that the process-thinking embedded in the method is valuable to enhance model content quality (i.e., relevance of the model), model presentation quality (i.e., comprehensibility and consistency of the model), and modelers' enjoyment of the modeling processes. Thus, there is a clear design-oriented recommendation for methods and tool that support seizing in process-oriented dynamic capabilities: These methods should be process-oriented.

## 5.2  Contributions to Practice

It is hoped that practitioners, e.g., decision makers or process managers, can make use of the results presented in this SpringerBrief. This section gives a general overview of the central contributions.

The developed process-oriented dynamic capability framework helps practitioners to understand and structure their BPM and service innovation endeavors. This is especially true with regards to collaboration, capability sourcing, and capability development. Regarding collaboration, the framework and especially its empirical applications suggest that collaboration with external actors (e.g., suppliers or customers) is beneficial and improves process-oriented dynamic capability success. This, in turn, improves the success of operational capabilities, e.g., processes or new services. With regards to capability sourcing, it can be argued that organizations in low dynamic market environments do not necessarily need the same quality of process-oriented dynamic capabilities in house. In contrast to organizations in high velocity markets, these organizations can rely on external actors and source their capabilities differently, e.g., from the market. This argument also helps to understand capability development. Practitioners should be very careful when applying maturity models. The presented results indicate that maturity models have certain insufficiencies with regards to the prescription of capability development. Here, the optimal level of capabilities should be carefully selected based on environmental characteristics and past organizational decisions.

Another important contribution to practice stems from the design-oriented parts. The method for the development of process-oriented business models ProcBiz and the corresponding OctoProz tool can be used by practitioners. Here, results from applications of the method and tool suggest that the process perspective in the method has certain advantages with regards to service innovation when compared to classical business modeling frameworks. Thus, practitioners choosing a business model framework should evaluate available options carefully. Often, the business model framework should be process-oriented as the resulting models are more comprehensible, consistent, and relevant. Moreover, the process-orientation has certain advantages with regards to information reuse in later activities (e.g., in later seizing and transformation). Of course, different individual preferences of the model designers might require organizations to let the designers choose the framework to use. However, ProcBiz has certain advantages with regards to the enjoyment of the model creation process which might influence the individual preferences of the modelers and, thus, their choice, too.

## 5.3  Limitations

Naturally, the presented research has some limitations. In the following, a short overview of the general limitations is given.

Firstly, most of the research was focused on Germany. This is not only true for all of the cases studied in the qualitative research parts, but also for the quantitative data set Service Firms, and the experimental evaluation of the design artifact. The only exception is the data set Local Administration which included Japanese organizations, too. Thus, the generalizability to other settings could be limited. This is especially true for settings with greater differences, e.g., settings in developing countries.

Secondly, the quantitative studies are both limited to certain sectors. One of the studies focuses on the public sector which naturally is quite different to other sectors (Niehaves et al. 2012). Furthermore, the other quantitative focuses on service organization and, thus, service innovation (Plattfaut et al. 2013a, b). Here, the generalizability of the results to other process-oriented dynamic capability might be difficult. However, the qualitative studies showed that BPM and service innovation could both be understood as process-oriented dynamic capabilities which supports the argument of generalizability of the quantitative results to BPM.

Thirdly, the generalization of process-oriented dynamic capabilities to dynamic capabilities in general is only possible to a certain extent. In how far other dynamic capabilities, e.g., new product development, alliancing, or research and development, can profit from the results of this publication was not in focus. Thus, this SpringerBrief is limited in this direction.

Lastly, qualitative research is always a matter of interpretation of the case data. Although most of the studies were conducted by multiple authors, perspectives on and interpretations of the case studies might differ to those derived by other authors or teams of authors. Thus, the results are, to a certain extent, subjective. This limitation was addressed through the multi-method research approach with the inclusion of further quantitative studies.

## 5.4 Future Research

This SpringerBrief opens up for future research. In the following, the six main areas of future research will be presented.

Firstly, the developed process-oriented dynamic capability framework can be further analyzed. While the framework could be used to understand BPM and service innovation, other process-oriented dynamic capabilities might exist, too. Their identification and analysis is open for future research. Moreover, the asset usage in process-oriented dynamic capabilities was only a secondary aspect. It is open for future research to analyze what assets (or classes of assets) help improve the success of process-oriented dynamic capabilities (or the corresponding abilities or activities). This could be achieved with the help of further case studies or quantitative surveys.

Secondly, with the understanding of BPM as a process-oriented dynamic capability, insufficiencies of classical BPM maturity models could be identified. However, this SpringerBrief did not provide alternatives to describe or prescribe ways of BPM capability development. Here, future research on BPM capability development models is necessary, e.g., in terms of case study research or action research. First results appear to be promising (Pöppelbuß 2012). Potentially, the results can be generalized to a process-oriented dynamic capability development model. However, this is also open for future research.

Thirdly, the collected quantitative data set Service Firms can be further analyzed. In the data set, data with regards to creativity support was collected. The analysis of this data was not in focus of this research and is currently work in progress. Moreover, the data can be analyzed with regards to different service sectors. Organizations from the data set Service Firms offer, e.g., IT-services, financial services, or public services. This differentiation calls for inter- and intra-sectoral research. As the development of dynamic capabilities depends on environmental dynamics and as environmental dynamics in turn depend on the sector, the derived variable of environmental dynamics could be included into the analysis, too.

Fourthly, further tests and applications of the developed method for process-oriented business modeling ProcBiz are needed. Here, especially evaluations and applications of the method in real life situations seem to be fruitful. Researchers could rely on methods like focus groups, action research, or case study research. This gap is currently tackled by the KollaPro research team. First applications of the method are promising.

Fifthly, next to the ProcBiz method, the implemented prototype OctoProz has to be tested further, too. As the prototypical implementation offers functionality a brown paper cannot offer (e.g., with regards to collaboration independent of time and location, support of business casing, or export to other IT artifacts such as Microsoft Excel or Software AG ARIS Business Architect), the tests should concentrate on these functionalities, too. Here, the KollaPro team is actively conducting first focus groups. However, other research method as case study research could be evaluated and eventually employed, too.

Lastly, future research could also focus on the limitations mentioned above. Here, researchers could replicate the studies in other settings (other sectors or geographic regions). Especially applications in developing countries or countries with other cultural background with regards to collaboration seem to be fruitful.

# References

Niehaves, B., Plattfaut, R., & Becker, J. (2012). Business process governance: A comparative study of Germany and Japan. *Business Process Management Journal, 18*(2), 347–371.

Plattfaut, R., Niehaves, B., Voigt, M., Malsbender, A., Ortbach, K., & Pöppelbuß, J. (2013a). IT and collaboration in service innovation: A dynamic capability perspective. In *Proceedings of the 21st European Conference for Information Systems (ECIS)*, Utrecht, Netherlands.

Plattfaut, R., Niehaves, B., Voigt, M., Malsbender, A., Ortbach, K., & Pöppelbuß, J. (2013b). *What makes service innovation successful? a dynamic capability perspective*, unpublished manuscript.

Pöppelbuß, J. (2012). *Business process management in service networks—capability assessment and improvement*. Dissertation. Wirtschaftswissenschaftliche Fakultät. Westfälische Wilhelms-Universität Münster.

# Chapter 6
# Conclusion

In this SpringerBrief, a theoretical framework for process-oriented dynamic capabilities was developed. This framework is able to serve as a basis for understanding and analyzing BPM and service innovation from a theoretical perspective. Thus, it is a valuable step in closing the existing research gap of a missing theoretical understanding of both concepts and serves as an answer to RQ.1. Next, the framework was applied in multiple case studies. Results suggest that the framework is valid and useful for analyzing BPM and service innovation in organizations. Here, several contributions could be identified. Moreover, the framework was used for two quantitative studies. Results show that collaboration and IT support both play an important role for the success of process-oriented dynamic capabilities. Thus, the developed process-oriented dynamic capability framework is valid and useful (ad RQ.2). Based on empirical applications of the theoretical framework a method for the creation of conceptual business models for the service industry (ProcBiz) was developed and implemented in a first software prototype (OctoProz). Both ProcBiz and OctoProz serve as answers to RQ.3.

The developed and empirically validated process-oriented dynamic capability framework that can be used to understand, structure, and analyze BPM and service innovation serves as the main contribution to theory. The developed method (ProcBiz) and the corresponding tool (OctoProz) are the main contributions to practice.

This publication is limited with regards to the choice of sector (mostly service industry) and country (mostly Germany). Moreover, the generalizability of BPM and service innovation to other process-oriented dynamic capabilities and to dynamic capabilities in general is up to future research. Other avenues of future research include further applications of ProcBiz and OctoProz, further analysis of the collected data set in the service industry, and further tests and applications of the process-oriented dynamic capability framework.

R. Plattfaut, *Process-Oriented Dynamic Capabilities*, SpringerBriefs in Information Systems, 57
DOI: 10.1007/978-3-319-03251-1_6, © The Author(s) 2014

# Appendix: Conceptual Meta-Model of ProcBiz

Meta-models are often used in IS research to describe modeling methods such as ProcBiz (Strahringer 1996). Meta-models describe the syntax, i.e., the modeling elements a language such as ProcBiz consists of and how these modeling elements can be combined with one another (Dietrich et al. 2013). Predominantly, meta-models are specified using the Entity-Relationship Notation (Chen 1976; Strahringer 1996). Meta-models can be used to compare different modeling languages and to create software artefacts implementing the modeling language (Strahringer 1996).

The conceptual meta-model of ProcBiz (Fig. A.1) describes the syntax of the language as explained in Sect. 4.5 and shown in Fig. 4.7 using Entity-Relationship Notation (Chen 1976). The prototypical software implementation OctoProz builds upon this meta-model.

Value propositions are either customer value propositions or business value propositions. They are delivered by one or more process elements. However, process elements do not necessarily have value propositions. Process elements are customer activities, business activities, or channels. They are ordered in a time-logical sequence. In this sequence, customer (business) activities are only followed by customer (business) activities or channels. Channels mediate between the customer and the business sphere and, thus, cannot be followed by another channel. Internal or external resources can be used to perform a process element. However, process elements not using resources might exist, too. Variable finance elements (i.e., costs when negative and revenue when positive) relate either directly to a process element or to the relationship between a process element and a resource. In this way, the costs of a specific resource used in a specific process step are modeled. Resources can also be used in central functions. These are business functions that are independent of one single service provision and, thus, not part of the process itself. Again, central functions and resources used by central functions can be associated with fixed finance elements (i.e., fixed costs or fixed revenues).

R. Plattfaut, *Process-Oriented Dynamic Capabilities*, SpringerBriefs in Information Systems, 59
DOI: 10.1007/978-3-319-03251-1, © The Author(s) 2014

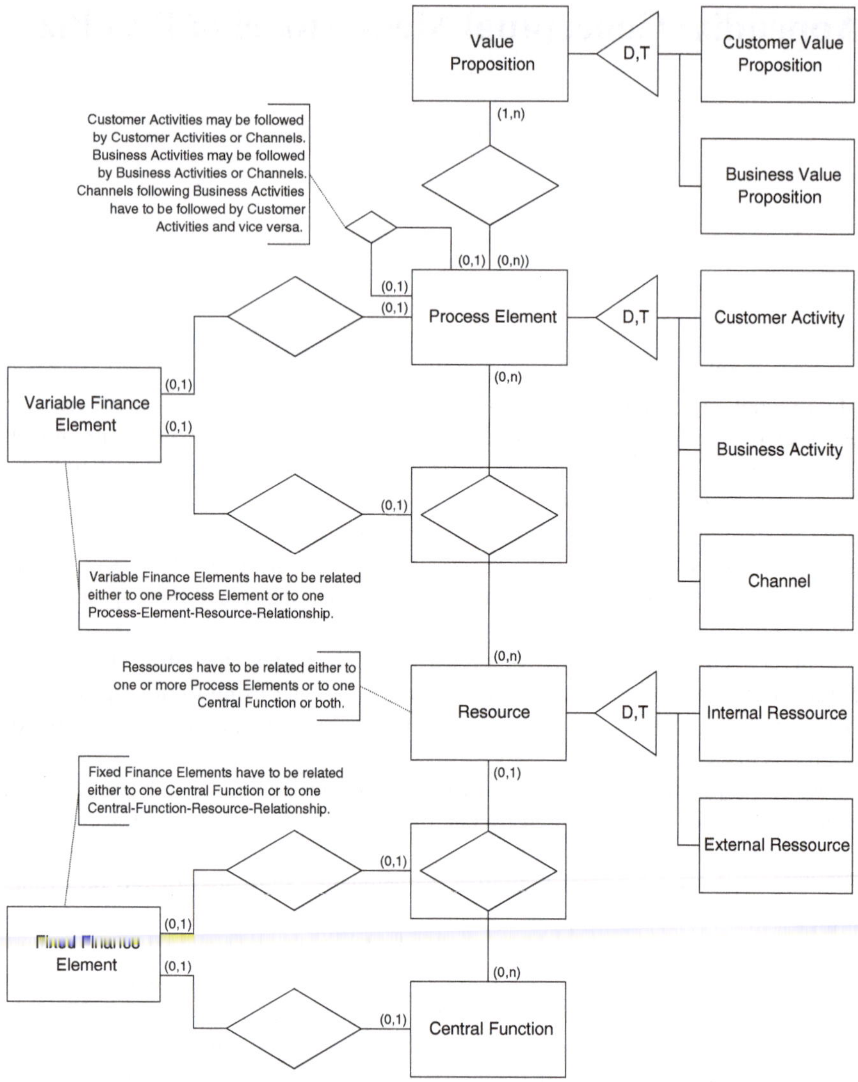

**Fig. A.1** Meta-Model of ProcBiz

# References

Chen, P. P. (1976). The entity-relationship model—toward a unified view of data. *ACM Transactions on Database Systems*, *1*(1), 9–36.

Dietrich, H.-A., Breuker, D., Steinhorst, M., Delfmann, P. & Becker, J. (2013). Developing graphical model editors for Meta-Modelling Tools-Requirements, Conceptualisation, and Implementation. *Enterprise Modelling and Information Systems Architectures*, *8*(2), (in press).

Strahringer, S. (1996). *Metamodellierung als Instrument Des Methodenvergleichs—Eine Evaluierung am Beispiel Objektorientierter Analysemethoden*. Aachen: Shaker Verlag.